Front Porch

❧ TALES ❧

Front Porch TALES

Philip Gulley

Multnomah Books
Sisters, Oregon

FRONT PORCH TALES

published by Multnomah Books
a part of the Questar publishing family

© 1997 by Philip Gulley

International Standard Book Number: 1-57673-123-5

Edited by Casandra Lindell
Copyedited by Candace McMahan
Cover photo by David Bailey Photography
Cover design by Kevin Keller
Illustrations by Cecil Rice

Printed in the United States of America

Scripture quotations are from the *Revised Standard Version* (RSV)
© 1946, 1952 by the Division of Christian Education
of the National Council of the Churches of Christ
in the United States of America

For information:
QUESTAR PUBLISHERS, INC.
POST OFFICE BOX 1720
SISTERS, OREGON 97759

Library of Congress Cataloging-in-Publication Data
Gulley, Philip.
    Front porch tales: a treasury of stories filled with wit and wisdom/by Philip
Gulley.   p.cm. ISBN 1-57673-123-5 (alk. paper) 1. Christian life-
Anecdotes. 2. Gulley, Philip. I. Title.
    BV4517.G85 1996   96-44879
    242--dc20   CIP

97 98 99 00 01 02 03 04 — 10 9 8 7 6 5 4 3 2

With gratitude to...

Joan, Spencer, and Sam Gulley,

who make our home such a gracious place to be,

and

Stan Banker, Jim Mulholland, and Tom Mullen,

whose encouragement and friendship I treasure,

and

the people of Irvington Friends Meeting,

who make me glad every day that I am their pastor.

THE CHURCH IN THE WILD WOOD

I don't know what I expected to find at the end of that narrow road through the bare trees in Marion County, Indiana, but what I found was a little red-brick church. A "meeting-house," the Quakers call it.

I went inside.

The place of worship was a room, plain and simple, with smooth tile floors and folding chairs facing a modest wooden pulpit. Behind this, sitting on a chair facing the others, was a man. Rather young, he seemed. Lean in face and frame. Hands clasped in his lap, head bowed slightly, eyes shut tightly, in obviously earnest prayer.

And the service of Friends began.

When the youthful pastor stood, the appearance of piety vanished. It was clear, in a quiet sort of way, that he loved these people in the folding chairs. And that they loved him. And as his eyes met theirs, I studied the former: large, brown, smiling, penetrating eyes. Something wonderful is about to happen, I thought.

And it did.

It was not a "speaker's voice," really. But it was warm and smooth, and it measured the words it spoke the way a journeyman carpenter measures wood. And so, one rafter, one casement at a time, did Philip Gulley craft for us in the folding chairs a house, of sorts, in which we dwelled for the next twenty minutes or so and which I have often happily revisited in my mind ever since.

To paraphrase him would paint a misshapen, colorless picture of that dear place he created for us. But I remember how what he said made me feel: as though I were drawn into a world for which I longed, and yet which I had believed was now inaccessible in these turbulent high-tech times. The tale he unveiled was tender and humorous, and the characters who populated it—real people whom the young pastor had known—came vividly to life as he spoke. And then, sudden, unexpected, lump-in-the-throat poignancy. And I found myself lamenting irresistibly that others who have longed, as I had, for once-upon-another-time did not know the way down the narrow road through the bare trees to the church in the wild wood and the gentle voice.

Well, now you do.

Paul Harvey Jr.

THE STORY BEHIND THESE STORIES

When I was in college, I took a course in English composition. I received a D, but only after promising the professor I would never write again. I laid down my pen and for ten years kept silent.

Then my Quaker meeting wanted a newsletter, and suddenly there was a front page which fell to me, the pastor, to fill. I began with stories. Stories of folks I had known and what I'd learned so far.

A woman in my meeting, Linda Baker, said, "You ought to write a book." So I drove over to the Earlham School of Religion and asked Tom Mullen to be my guide. And I asked my two best friends, Stan Banker and Jim Mulholland, to read my work. And I asked my wife, Joan, if she would mind doing the supper dishes and giving our sons their baths while I went down to the basement to write about family life. And they all agreed. So I settled in and wrote a book.

Then Paul Harvey Jr. and Dina Kinnan showed up one Sunday at our small Quaker meeting with Dina's sister, Denise. And Paul Jr. and Dina sent my manuscript to John Van Diest of Questar Publishers. And they agreed to publish it. So that's the story behind these stories.

I am profoundly grateful to all who had a hand in it—from Linda to John to you, the reader, for spending your hard-earned money on an unknown. And I'm grateful for my little Quaker meeting, who encourage me and pray for me and hold me in God's light.

Be aware that a few of the names and events in this book have been altered to protect persons still living, namely me. The alternative is full disclosure, which means I couldn't go back home for Swap and Shop Days or music nights at Ellis Park. Thomas Wolfe was mistaken. We can go home again. But not if we tell the whole, unvarnished truth. If you're from a small town, you'll understand what I mean.

Philip Gulley

CONTENTS

Folks I've Known

I live in a neighborhood full of children. I never knew there were children around until school began and I saw them waiting for the bus. Outside of school, they stay in their homes and play Nintendo. I don't know any of their names. I seldom see them ride their bikes or play football or baseball. I keep waiting for them to come around and play in the meeting-house yard, but they seldom do. So it sits empty. We laid out a baseball diamond, hoping kids would get the message. But vines grew up and nature reclaimed it before the feet of little children could wear it bare.

I thank God I was born before Nintendo and video games and all the other things that keep kids from getting out and exploring their environs. My parents turned off the television set and sent me outdoors, where I met all kinds of interesting people, like Mrs. Harvey and Doctor Gibbs and Mr. Welty.

Knowing these people was an education in and of itself. Sometimes people ask me when and where I started preparing for ministry. I tell them I was ten years old and that it was in Doctor Gibbs' yard, the day he was beating his saplings with a rolled-up newspaper.

Here is his story and the stories of other folks
I've known. I hope you are as blessed by reading
about these fine people as I was by knowing
them.

Growing Roots

Had an old neighbor when I was growing up named Doctor Gibbs. He didn't look like any doctor I'd ever known. Every time I saw him, he was wearing denim overalls and a straw hat, the front brim of which was green sunglass plastic. He smiled a lot, a smile that matched his hat—old and crinkly and well-worn. He never yelled at us for playing in his yard. I remember him as someone who was a lot nicer than circumstances warranted.

When Doctor Gibbs wasn't saving lives, he was planting trees. His house sat on ten acres, and his life-goal was to make it a forest. The good doctor had some interesting theories concerning plant husbandry. He came from the "No pain, no gain" school of horticulture. He never watered his new trees, which flew in the face of conventional wisdom. Once I asked why. He said that watering plants spoiled them, and that if you water them, each successive tree generation will grow weaker and weaker. So you have to make things rough for them and weed out the weenie trees early on.

He talked about how watering trees made for shallow roots, and how trees that weren't watered had to grow deep roots in search of moisture. I took him to mean that deep roots were to be treasured.

So he never watered his trees. He'd plant an oak and, instead of watering it every morning, he'd beat it with a rolled up newspaper. Smack! Slap! Pow! I asked him why he did that, and he said it was to get the tree's attention.

Doctor Gibbs went to glory a couple years after I left home. Every now and again, I walk by his house and look at the trees that I'd watched him plant some twenty-five years ago. They're granite strong now. Big and robust. Those trees wake up in the morning and beat their chests and drink their coffee black.

I planted a couple trees a few years back. Carried water to them for a solid summer. Sprayed them. Prayed over them. The whole nine yards. Two years of coddling has resulted in trees that expect to be waited on hand and foot. Whenever a cold wind blows in, they tremble and chatter their branches. Sissy trees.

Funny thing about those trees of Doctor Gibbs. Adversity and deprivation seemed to benefit them in ways comfort and ease never could.

Every night before I go to bed, I go check on my two sons. I stand over them and watch their little bodies, the rising and falling of life within. I often pray for them. Mostly I pray that their lives will be easy. "Lord, spare them from hardship." But lately I've been thinking that it's time to change my prayer.

Has to do with the inevitability of cold winds that hit us at the core. I know my children are going to encounter hardship, and my praying they won't is naive. There's always a cold wind blowing somewhere.

So I'm changing my eventide prayer. Because life is tough, whether we want it to be or not. Instead, I'm going to pray that my sons' roots grow deep, so they can draw strength from the hidden sources of the eternal God.

Too many times we pray for ease, but that's a prayer seldom met. What we need to do is pray for roots that reach deep into the Eternal, so when the rains fall and the winds blow, we won't be swept asunder.

The Front Porch Classroom

When I was in the fourth grade, I was offered a job as a paper boy. It didn't pay much money, but I knew having a job would build my character so I took it, good character being important to fourth-graders. My lessons started the first day on the job. A customer paying his bill asked me if I wanted a tip, and I said, "Sure." He said, "Stay away from wild women."

One of my customers was a lady named Mrs. Stanley. She was a widow and not prone to wild living, so I took to lingering on her front porch during my rounds. She'd watch for me to come down her street, and by the time I'd pedaled up to her house, there'd be a slushy bottle of Coke waiting for me. I'd sit and drink while she talked. That was our understanding—I drank, she talked.

The widow Stanley talked mostly about her dead husband, Roger. "Roger and I went grocery shopping this morning over to the IGA," she'd say. The first time she said that, the Coke went up my nose. That was back in the days when Coke going up your nose wasn't a crime, just a mite uncomfortable.

Went home and told my father about Mrs. Stanley and how she talked as if Mr. Stanley were still alive. Dad said she was probably lonely, and that maybe I just ought to sit and listen and nod my head and smile, and maybe she'd work it out of her system. So that's what I did. I figured this was where the character-building came into play. Turned out Dad was right. After a few summers, she seemed content to leave her husband over at the South Cemetery.

Nowadays, we'd send Mrs. Stanley to a psychiatrist. But all she had back then was a front porch rocker and her paper boy's ear, which turned out to be enough.

I quit my paper route after her healing. Moved on to the lucrative business of lawn mowing. Didn't see the widow Stanley for several years. Then we crossed paths up at the Christian Church's annual fund-raiser dinner. She was standing behind the steam table spooning out mashed potatoes and looking radiant. Four years before she'd had to bribe her paper boy with a Coke to have someone to talk with;

now she had friends brimming over. Her husband was gone, but life went on. She had her community and was luminous with love.

Community is a beautiful thing; sometimes it even heals us and makes us better than we would otherwise be.

I live in the city now. My front porch is a concrete slab. And my paper boy is a lady named Edna with three kids and a twelve-year-old Honda. Every day she asks me how I'm doing. When I don't say "fine," she sticks around long enough to find out why. She's such a nice lady that sometimes I act as if I have a problem, just so she'll tarry. She's lived in the city all her life, but she knows about community, too.

Community isn't so much a locale as it is a state of mind. You find it whenever folks ask how you're doing because they care, and not because they're getting paid to inquire.

Two thousand years ago, a church elder named Peter wrote the recipe for community. "Above all else," he wrote, "hold unfailing your love for one another, since love covers a multitude of sins" (1 Peter 4:8). That means when you love a person, you occasionally have to turn a blind eye toward their shortcomings.

Kind of like what my Dad told me about the

widow Stanley. Sometimes it's better to nod your head and smile.

Psychiatrists call that "enabling denial," but back when I delivered papers, we called it "compassion."

When the Tree Went Crashing

A friend of mine has a bunch of college degrees. I was really impressed until he told me he was going to another city to deliver a paper. Heck, I was delivering papers in the fourth grade. One of my customers was a Quaker widow named Mrs. Harvey. When weather permitted, she'd sit on her front porch swing, waiting for the paper and a conversation. I'd pull up a rocking chair, and we'd sit and visit underneath the shade of the maple tree which stood guard over the porch.

One day she asked me if I would work as her yard boy. She had a big yard, almost two acres, which she wanted mowed with a push mower since riding mowers didn't do a very good job. She was emphatic about that and, since I didn't have a riding mower, I agreed with her.

I'd stop by every afternoon when I was done delivering papers and mow a section. Every afternoon but Sunday, since Mrs. Harvey said that was the Sabbath, and if the Lord needed to rest on the seventh day, who was I to work?

It was in the fourth year of my mowing that I noticed the front porch maple tree was dying. It had some years on it. Mr. and Mrs. Harvey had moved there the first year of their marriage, forty years before. Mr. Harvey had planted it then. "Twenty years from now, we'll appreciate this," he'd said at the time. And twenty years later they did appreciate it, on a summer evening when the heat would loosen its grip.

But after forty years, Mr. Harvey was dead, and so was the tree. And when I told Mrs. Harvey, she stared at the tree the longest time and told how she still remembered what her husband was wearing when he planted that tree. Then she went in her house and called Kenny. He was the man in our town who cut trees.

He rolled up the next day in his truck and got right down to business—another day, another tree. Mrs. Harvey was watching from her front porch swing, along with her neighbor, who had made her way over to offer comfort. So when the chain saw bit into the tree and Mrs. Harvey flinched, her neighbor took her hand and listened while Mrs. Harvey talked about summer evenings that were supposed to be but never were.

Once spent a whole semester studying the book of Job. Never did understand it until I read it in light of Mrs. Harvey.

Job had it all, then Job lost it all. Servants: murdered. Wealth: stolen. Health: gone. Sons and daughters and bounce-on-your-knee grandchildren: dead. Job sat on a pile of ashes, lamenting over a life that was supposed to be, but never was. God made his way over to Job and sat with him amidst the charred remains of his life. A tender thing, given the immensity of the universe and the smallness of Job. But then God knows our secret pain.

When I was in college, my philosophy professor spent an entire week talking about love. But for me it was never clearer than the day the tree went crashing.

Expectation

Was over visiting my folks one autumn morning, and Ray stopped by to borrow Dad's car. Dad and Ray became friends when Dad served on the town board and met Ray, who worked for the sewer department. Ray's one of those eminently useful men it pays to know if you need something done—from getting a raccoon out of your attic to nosing out the most likely spots for morel mushrooms to setting off the town fireworks on the Fourth of July. In a specialist world, Ray's a generalist, which inclines me to think well of him. The problem today is that too many folks know a lot about a thing or two, but not enough folks know a little about a lot of things. If you don't believe that, just try to find a doctor who'll mend your feet and your nose in the same visit.

Ray started working for the town when he graduated from high school. College was out of the question, it costing money and Ray not having any. Instead, he married his high school sweetheart. They settled into a small house outside of town and slipped into the lifestyle Ray had come from—work, raise your kids, hope they turn out right, and pray to Jesus that Social Security is still around when you retire. And every now and then, lying awake at night frustrated that your kids can't have the same things the doctor's children have.

Ray and his wife had a first-born daughter who hit school like a cyclone. Made straight As, which startled the teachers, she being Ray's daughter. It wasn't that Ray lacked enthusiasm for learning; he just wasn't one to let school get in the way of his education. His interests lay elsewhere. I'm that way myself. Took me to eighth grade to figure out that algebra wasn't a line of Playtex undergarments.

Ray's daughter kept up her grades. Outhustled the doctor's kid to become the class valedictorian. But the halls of Harvard don't overflow with sewer worker offspring, so she was trying to get used to the idea of a career in fast food. Then a college in Ohio, scouting around for smart kids with gumption, offered her a free education, and her dream of being a psychologist drew closer. So she went to Ohio, and Ray, whose truck kicks up a fuss when driven past the county line, borrows my Dad's car once a month to go visit his daughter, of whom he is fiercely proud.

There's a heap of people pulling for that young lady. Lot of folks who stop Ray on the street to ask how she's doing. When she went to Ohio, she carried a passel of expectation with her. If she fails, the entire town will lose its will to live. Other than that, I don't think she's under much pressure.

Some people would crumble under her heavy weight of expectation. But what would crush others seems only to enliven her. What I'm betting is that ten years from now she'll be charging a doctor's kid two hundred dollars a session to help get his head on straight. He'll moan about how his parents expected too much, and she'll tell him to grow up and get a life—in a therapeutic way, of course, and with appropriate sensitivity. Then the next time she sees her dear old parents, she'll give them a hug and whisper, "Thanks for believing in me."

She's learning early on what takes most of us a whole lifetime to uncover—that expectation is a blessing, not a curse. It's a beautiful thing when people expect something decent of you. It means you've given them reason for confidence. Like when John the Baptist was born and his father sang a beautiful song about all the things his boy would do. Then his boy went out and did them.

Many a powerful life have their starts in expectation.

Doc Foster

I once visited a friend in New York City. We drove around the city, taking in the sights. It was a grand place and, though I wouldn't want to live there, I am the richer for my brief stay. A most impressive thing happened the evening I slept at my friend's apartment. His wife asked him to take out the garbage. He invited me to watch him. Having carried out trash myself, I wasn't all that excited at the prospect but went along for the sake of politeness.

He took the trash to the end of his hallway, opened a little door, and dropped the trash in. There was a whooshing sound and the trash was gone, just like that. He explained how a vacuum system sucked up all the trash and carried it away. Remarkable.

When I was growing up in Danville, our trash-removal system was not as flashy, but it was just as reliable. His name was Doc Foster, and for a dollar a week he pulled up at our curb in his pickup truck, climbed out, threw our trash in the back, and drove away. If we forgot to set our trash out, he'd drive back to our barn and get it himself. When he had a truck full he'd drive out to the town dump on Twin Bridges Road, unload, wet his finger, and put it in the air; if the wind wasn't blowing toward town, he'd commence to burning.

Doc Foster was black, the only black man in our town. He lived just south of the lumberyard across the railroad tracks all by himself. I hate to think his skin color dictated where he lived, though I suspect it did, and am to my core ashamed that the first thing we noticed about Doc was his color.

In other ways, our town rose to splendid heights when it came to Doc. On his seventy-seventh birthday, we held a surprise party for him in the rotunda of the courthouse. That had never been done before, at least in my memory, and hasn't been done since. Except when President Reagan came to town and we had a big celebration for him. Personally, I think Doc Foster did a whole lot more for Danville than any president ever did.

Back in the 1930s, during the Depression days, we had a teacher's college in our town. Doc would often pass along a little extra tuition money to struggling students, and in this way helped supply our town with a fresh crop of teachers.

In addition to hauling trash and being a friend to man, Doc made himself available for a whole host of tasks, from raking leaves to mowing lawns. His truck bristled with brooms and rakes of all sizes and shapes. When out-of-town visitors would compliment us for our town's cleanliness, we would swell with pride as if we ourselves had swept up the trash the dogs had scattered. Doc did what all good people do— made the rest of us look better than we really were.

Doc Foster died in the winter of '89. The day of the funeral it was snowing and not many people showed up to pay their respects. My father went and is to this very day saddened that more folks didn't make their way through a little snow to honor a man who never let foul weather keep him from his appointed rounds. I prefer to remember how a town gathered in a courthouse rotunda and celebrated a man's contribution while he was still alive to enjoy their praise.

On the back wall at our Quaker meeting-house hangs a banner listing the fruit of the Spirit—love, joy, peace, patience, kindness, goodness, faithfulness, gentleness, and self-control. When I try to think of what that looks like, my mind returns to a man who found dignity in hauling trash and sweeping gutters. What a gift his memory is to me.

I didn't tell this to my New York friend. What I told him was how remarkable his trash collection system was and how lucky he was to have it. Though I knew the finer blessing was mine.

The Paper Route

*I*f you want to learn about life, you can go to college and study psychology, or you can take a paper route. I did the latter while in the fourth grade for the princely sum of seven dollars a week. As paper routes go, mine was small with only twenty-six customers. My friend Bill Eddy had upwards of eighty customers and three times the income, though he was so frazzled, the larger wage seemed hardly worth the struggle. Bill needed the extra money to finance his pinball playing at Danner's Five and Dime.

Having a limited clientele allowed me to learn the peculiarities of each.

Mr. Willard wanted his paper under the brick on the front porch chair so the wind wouldn't scatter it. He got home late and didn't want to have to chase his paper down Washington Street.

The lawyer Vandivier wanted me to hand the paper to his secretary, Miss Dillow. She was so nice and pretty, I didn't mind a bit. When I grew old enough to start dating girls, I compared every one to Miss Dillow but became discouraged when few could match her charms.

Mrs. Carter was a widow with two "slow" children. She worked as a waitress at the Coffee Cup and always had a hard time paying her bill. One day I went to collect and she had moved away owing more than four dollars, more than half my week's pay. That's when I learned that not paying your bills causes somebody somewhere hardship.

The Blakes were some of the poorest people on my paper route. They were also the most generous and would often give extravagant tips—fifty cents and more. They depended on tips to get by in their jobs and thus were sensitive to the working class. I would like to banish tips altogether and pay higher prices so folks can enjoy a living wage. It's terrible to have to provide for your family with a job that relies so heavily upon a fickle thing like human generosity. Anyone who works forty hours a week shouldn't have to depend on tips to fill their children's stomachs.

Miss Myna Towells wanted me to ring her doorbell and hand the paper to her, which I would do. She would thank me and close the door. Every Christmas she tipped precisely one dollar. She pinched her hair up in a tight, black bun. She never married, though I kept hoping some man in a red convertible would spirit her away and bring vigor to her stale life. When I later read that single people don't live as long as married people, I thought of Miss Towells and wasn't surprised.

One of my customers was an elderly man who came to the door wearing women's dresses. He never offered an explanation, and I never asked for one. Small towns aren't always the bastions of conformity we think they are.

Mr. Day was a chain smoker and would sit on his porch in a swirl of blue smoke. You could hear him cough a block away. He was fifty years old when I started delivering his paper. He told me how he began smoking when he was fourteen and how it never hurt him. The next year he came down with emphysema and traded in his cigarettes for an oxygen tank and hospital bed.

If I had had eighty customers, I would never have gotten to know all these people and their idiosyncrasies. I would have been consigned to a bicycle, flinging papers at porches as I whizzed by. Instead, I climbed off my bike and shook hands and learned of a wider world.

It established a pattern for living which I've tried diligently to maintain—bigger isn't always better, more money means more worries, and knowing people beats knowing about them.

Streams in the Desert

Went over to my folks' house one spring day to celebrate my nephew's first birthday. Took a walk and saw people out working in their yards, folks I hadn't seen for years. I saw Mr. Amos Welty down on the corner, raking up the winter deadfall from his yard. Getting the place ready for six months of flowers, starting with the crocuses and ending with the mums. His crocuses were up. I stopped to look at them. He came over to talk, which made me nervous, since we had parted enemies twenty years before.

Mr. Welty had been a sour man, a mean man, truth be told. Once, he even threw a shovel at me for walking on his grass. I upped the ante the next day by nailing him with a water balloon. He was pulling weeds, stood to stretch, and I caught him amidships—POW!

He called the town police officer, Charlie Morelock, who put out an all-points bulletin on me. Officer Morelock found me in my front yard. He stopped his cruiser, climbed out, and walked toward me with his hand on his gun. He drew near, reached out, laid his heavy hand on my shoulder, looked me in the eye, and said, "Good shot." He didn't like Mr. Welty either.

So I hadn't talked with Mr. Welty since that time, but it was on my mind when he walked toward me that early spring day. He extended his hand and we shook, which disarmed me. Then we talked about crocuses and other harbingers of spring.

Twenty years ago, he was corroded with anger; now he was gentleness personified. He had changed. Amos Welty had metamorphosed. I talked with my dad about it. He said Mr. Welty has been nice ever since his mother died. She was all he had, then she died and he was alone. It occurred to him that instead of throwing shovels at children, he should invite them to his porch for bubble gum and cookies. Now his yard has bare spots where grass once grew, but it seems a far lovelier place.

Read a book that said one's personality and character are pretty well formed by the age of five. By then folks can tell whether someone will be sipping Ripple in an alleyway or inventing a cure for cancer. At least that's what the author of this book said—get it right in five years or start saving for bail money.

I pitched the book. First, because I didn't need the pressure. I have two children and a spastic colon, so I already don't sleep nights. But I also pitched it because I know too many Mr. Weltys—folks who changed horses midway across life's stream. Got tired of the nag of hate they were riding and traded up to charity and grace.

The prophet Isaiah talks about God making streams in the desert. Talks about how God puts things where they've never been before, like love where hate once reigned. Streams in the desert, Isaiah calls it.

I'm here to tell you these streams are real, for early one spring, when the crocuses bloomed, I waded into one.

My Grandma, the Saint

I want to confess my prejudice right up front by declaring unequivocally that my Grandma Norma was the sweetest lady who ever lived. I didn't realize this until she had passed away, which explains why I drove by her house sometimes without stopping to visit.

She was past ninety when she died. Stumbled off the back porch, broke her hip, and died four days after the operation that was supposed to make her as good as new. I suspect she overheard the doctor say "nursing home" and simply willed herself to die. Technically, her heart gave out, which makes sense, knowing how much she used it.

Grandma was the family antidote to the both-parents-working-and-too-tired-to-talk syndrome. Since this isn't an essay about how we have to work so much because we want so much, I won't dwell on that. I'll only say that Grandma decided early on that being there for children was more important than working to buy them stuff they didn't need in the first place.

Psychiatrists have the couch, but Grandma had the porch swing and the kitchen table and a certain way of listening as if you were the only one in God's world worth hearing. Lot of talk these days about the formation of self-esteem and helping children feeling valued, but we want the schools to do it. I remember when an hour with Grandma left you feeling like royalty.

Given her prospects, I understood her wanting to cross heaven's threshold. Only thing is, she stepped over before we were done needing her. I wanted my sons to do some swing time with her. Wanted them to hear how there was no one quite like them, and how special they were and handsome and smart. The kind of things Grandma told me. Now I guess it falls to my mom. I wonder if she knows that, or if I'll have to tell her. I suspect she knows, being Grandma's daughter.

I call my grandmother a saint because she's the only person I ever met who prayed her rosary twice a day. Those were the only times she wasn't available to us, when she was in her bedroom lifting up her "Hail Marys" and "Our Fathers." As a child, I resented the notion that talking with God was more important than talking with me.

In retrospect, I understand that time she spent in prayer helped her be all the more present for others. Maybe the reason we don't have time for one another anymore isn't because we work too much, but because we pray too little. How else can God reorder our priorities?

At her funeral, the priest said it was a day of celebration. That's the kind of thing we ministers learn to say in seminary. And it holds up until someone like Grandma dies, then no amount of heaven-talk eases the pain. The graveyard sees a hurt the classroom never knows.

In the Bible it tell us not to worry, that in God's house are found mansions aplenty. I don't think Grandma would like a mansion. Too much dusting. Just give her a porch swing and a child needing love. And throw in a breeze which blows in from the old days, when an hour with a saint made all the world right.

My Grandpa, the Enigma

My grandpa was born in 1904 in the Belgian village of Gosselies. His name is Henry, which is where I got my middle name. People call him Hank. Sometimes we call him Hank the Crank. That's because he can be grouchy. He can also be loving and gentle. Which is why I call him an enigma.

Grandpa moved to America when he was a little kid. He and his family came through Ellis Island. They moved to West Virginia, and his father worked in the glass factories. Grandpa started school in West Virginia. Like most immigrant families, Grandpa's family was intensely proud. Never admit you need help with anything. They sent Grandpa to school even though he couldn't speak a word of English. Today he speaks as well as you or I, though sometimes I catch a trace of Gosselies village in his voice.

Grandpa was the oldest son in his family. Sometimes his parents weren't all that gentle—

quicker with a swat than a hug. When he was ready to enter the sixth grade, his father said the books cost too much. So he pulled Grandpa out of school, took him to the foreman down at the glass factory, and signed a paper saying Grandpa was sixteen. Grandpa went to work fulltime. He was thirteen years old. He gave his paychecks to his parents. The week before he and Grandma were married, his parents let him keep his paycheck. That's what families from Gosselies did back then.

They had three girls. My mother was one of them, along with my Aunt Cathy and Aunt Mary. When Mom was six, she had her tonsils taken out. Grandpa showed up at the hospital with a catcher's mitt for her. He also gave her a BB gun. He never said so, but sometimes I think he wanted a son.

When World War II came along, he sold the car and bought all the family brand-new bicycles since gasoline was hard to come by. Mom has a picture of them sitting on their new bikes. Considering a war was on, they looked happy. They rode the bikes everywhere—to Knowles Market and to church. Grandpa walked to work. He still worked at the glass factory, just like his father.

When he was in his early fifties, the glass factory closed down. They didn't need people to cut glass anymore, since machines could do it. Grandpa got a job working with an architect. He'd taken drafting classes at night. He designed school additions. Then he got a job selling school equipment and traveled all over southern Indiana. After working in a factory since the age of thirteen, he enjoyed getting out and meeting people.

When I was growing up, we'd go visit Grandpa. The first thing he'd say when he saw us was, "Hello, good to see you. When you going home?" Then he'd take me out to his workshop and teach me how to work with wood. Whenever I made a mistake, he'd get impatient and take the tool away. But when we went back in the house he'd tell Mom and Dad I did just fine.

After sixty-seven years of marriage, Grandma died. Grandpa lives with a little dog named Babe. Babe still goes to Grandma's bedroom every morning to see if she's come home from wherever it is she went. I go visit Grandpa, but not as often as I'd like. The last time I went, he took me out to his workshop to show me his new table saw. He told me it'll last ten or fifteen years. He's ninety-one. I hope it goes before he does.

Ruby and the Rain Crow

My mother-in-law, Ruby Apple, lives on a farm in southern Indiana. She's lived there since before World War II, in a house whose two front rooms used to be a grain crib. A man with a tractor pulled the grain crib over from Grandpa Linus' home place. She and her husband, Howard, bought some dairy cows and chickens and sold milk and eggs to the dairy. Ruby remembers lying in bed at night and listening to the eggs crack after her wood stove lost its battle with the winter cold.

Ruby and Howard had three boys, waited eleven years, then had two girls. Howard used to say they were the best crop they ever raised. The boys went to a one-room school. Poor, disadvantaged things. No swimming pool during gym class, no teacher fretting over their self-esteem. Not knowing any better, the boys went off to college, got degrees, and made something of themselves. Then danged if those two girls didn't go and do the same.

Ruby and Howard had a straightforward parenting philosophy—hard work, good food, lots of love, and church on Sundays. They also had the good sense to live beyond the range of most television stations, so the reception was pitiful. They watched *Hee Haw* on Saturday nights, but Grandpa Jones was always upside down and green. A little of that went a long way.

Howard died in 1975. Ruby sold off the farm equipment, learned to drive, and took a job in town caring for an old man and his wife. The girls went to college, got married, and started families of their own. None of the kids wants to live there, so when Ruby dies, one hundred and fifty years of Apples living on that old gravel road will come to end. I try not to think about that.

I go down to visit Ruby every now and again. We get in the car and drive down toward the old Grimes' place and past the Roscoe Bennet farm. We stop at the Apple Chapel graveyard where those one hundred and fifty years' worth of Apples are buried. Ruby knows the story of each one. When she dies, that will come to an end too.

One day I was visiting, and Ruby called me to the window.

"Listen to that," she said. I listened and heard a bird give five short "whooo's."

"What is it?" I asked.

"A rain crow," she said. "You hear them before a big rain. I've never seen one, but I've heard them plenty of times."

That was a new one on me, but I wasn't about to argue with Ruby. If she says there are birds that call out five "whooo's" before a big rain, birds she's never laid eyes on, the smart money is on Ruby. It rained two hours later.

The Gospel of John tells about the resurrected Jesus visiting the disciples, and Thomas not believing it was Jesus until he touched the wounds. John tells how Jesus said, "Blessed are those who have not seen and yet believe" (John 20:29). A lot of smart people say John wrote at a time when the folks who had known Jesus were dead and gone. So John told this story to reassure early Christians that you can believe in something you've never seen. Kind of like Ruby believes in the rain crows.

We're all Missourians at heart, inclined toward the "show-me!" Except every now and then we bump into Jesus and rain crows, where seeing doesn't come easy. Then the only thing to do is listen for the still, small voice, and the five short "whooo's" to know there's substance beyond the seeing.

Sometimes the most real things are the things we cannot see.

My Friend Jim and Why I Don't Like Him

My friend Jim is a minister. He wears a big cross. He gives a wad of money away every year. He is devout. He is smart. His children are gifted, and his wife mows the lawn. Naturally, I despise him.

Once he went on a trip to Honduras. "A mission trip," he told me, "to minister to the poor." It was the middle of winter, of course, when God routinely calls us to minister in the tropics.

He needed work boots for the trip, so I lent him a pair of mine. I have two pairs of boots— my motorcycle boots and my snow-shoveling boots. My motorcycle boots are the John Waynes of footwear. I pull those babies on, and small children cower behind their mothers' skirts. No one, I repeat, no one wears them but me. My snow-shoveling boots are part of the Ward Cleaver collection. Thankfully, I haven't had to wear them since convincing my wife that shoveling snow actually melts fat from the hips and thighs. Jim got those.

I drove Jim to the airport. He had never flown before and was nervous, so I comforted him by pointing out that death by airplane crash, though increasingly common, was virtually painless.

Jim was gone for three weeks. He called on the phone when he got back home. "I have good news and bad news," he said. "The bad news is that the airline lost all my luggage, including your boots. The good news is that the airline says they're sure to find everything." They still call him every week to report on their progress. Naturally, Jim and I remain confident that the airline will pursue this matter with the same thorough efficiency we've come to expect from them.

There are losses, and there are losses. Whenever I see Jim, I reminisce aloud about the best pair of boots I'd ever had, but the truth is, I haven't missed them at all. I lost them, but they were not a loss. But my grandmother Norma died right before that, and it was an uppercut to the heart. It felt like a thief broke in and stole the family quilt and ripped out the center pieces. So there are losses, then there are losses.

Once heard a psychologist talking about loss. She said most folks she counsels are folks who suffered loss—loss of a loved one, loss of innocence, loss of trust—before they were capable of dealing with it. Sometimes we lose things before we're done needing them.

Story in the Bible tells about a man who lost a prodigal son. The other side of that story was about a son who lost a father. Then it hit him that maybe his father wasn't lost to him after all, and he swallowed pride and headed for home.

My friend Jim says pride can cause us to lose a lot of things, like perspective and faith and compassion. He's right, of course, like he is about most things, which, if you must know, is why I don't like him. But I'm working on it.

Tim

I met Tim in the second grade. We sat together in Mrs. Worrel's class. We became friends when we discovered no other group would have us. We weren't athletic enough to be jocks. The girls didn't like us because we looked funny. Even the Scouts, who had taken a solemn oath to be kind and charitable, steered clear of us.

Tim lived on a farm. I lived in town. When we hit fourth grade, our parents let us ride our bikes back and forth to each other's houses. Our social life increased exponentially. On Fridays, Tim would ride in to my house to spend the night. We'd go to the movies up at the Royal Rathole. The jocks would sit near the back and neck with the girls, and we'd sit behind them and make kissing noises.

On Saturdays, I'd ride my Schwinn Varsity out to Tim's. We'd stay up late to watch *Planet of the Apes*. His mom was a night-shift nurse at the county hospital. She'd bring us a tray of Cokes and Pringles, give us both a good night kiss, and head into work. She was real nice. A lot of mothers don't like having extra kids around, but she never seemed to mind. I always felt welcome. I'm going to try and remember that when my boys start bringing their friends home.

When we were in the eighth grade, I invited a girl named Amy to the spring dance. Tim came along. We wore plaid leisure suits and drank a lot of punch. Amy spent most of her time in the bathroom.

Then we went to high school. We took all the same classes so we could be together. We were both girl crazy. Unfortunately, our feelings weren't reciprocated. The prettiest girl in school was named Laura. She was a cheerleader, and Tim loved her. She was a friend of my brother's, who was a jock, so I asked her for her picture. She signed it "to someone I really admire." I think it's because she didn't remember my name. I sold it to Tim for two bucks. Friendship had its limits.

When we graduated from high school, we got jobs. I worked in an office for an electric utility. Tim was a mechanic at Logan's Mobil. I'd stop by every morning on my way to work for a dollar's worth of gas and conversation. Then at night we'd get in his car and drive to McDonald's in the next town over.

Flush with money from our jobs, we decided to buy motorcycles. Tim bought one that had a custom paint job. It didn't run well, but it looked good. We'd ride every Sunday afternoon and most nights. A lot of times we'd end up at the Dairy Queen, where we'd sit on our bikes and talk about stuff that doesn't seem too important now, but was incredibly so then.

One night, about two o'clock, I got a phone call from the sheriff's chaplain, Joe Stump. He told me my best friend since Mrs. Worrel's second grade class had been hit by a drunken driver and was dead. They were afraid I had been hit too, so they were calling to check on me.

Tim's funeral was three days later. I was a pallbearer and sat on the front row. His parents sat across from me. His mother was a knot of grief; his dad bent and weighed. We buried him at the South Cemetery. All I remember now is the crying.

There are a lot of things about Tim I've forgotten. I do remember that he liked *The Dukes of Hazzard* and that he was taking a correspondence course on how to be a diesel mechanic. I remember his laugh. And I remember that in the fourteen years of our friendship, I never once heard him ridicule anyone.

When Tim died, a lot of people took it upon themselves to explain to me why it happened. I would listen and smile and nod my head, mostly so they'd go away and leave me alone.

There are some things about this life I'll never understand. One of them is why a drunken driver dies of old age when a never-hurt-a-flea young man barely sees twenty. Someday, I'm going to see God face to face. And when I do, I'm going to ask Him why that is.

The Wizard of Is

When my wife and I first married, we took a big camping trip every summer. We started out camping in a little tent, which worked fine, until one trip it rained five straight days and we went stir crazy. We saved our money and bought a bigger tent. It had two rooms, and we enjoyed the extra space. Then we loaned it to my sister. She packed it away wet, the seams rotted, and the tent fell apart. My sister does things like this, and there isn't much that can be done about it—other than to remind her of it whenever we need someone to watch the kids.

Camping is a holdover from my growing up days. There were five kids in my family, and camping was the only vacation Mom and Dad could afford. Had we been able to afford other kinds of vacations, we kids still would have chosen camping, it being high adventure.

Someone once told me that we don't remember days, we remember moments. What I recollect are moments gone but treasured. I'm six years old, camping with my family, and I catch my first fish on a Zebco rod and reel. Dad takes a picture, which is unearthed twenty-five years later on a Thanksgiving afternoon when my brother David hauls the picture-box down from the attic. My three-year-old climbs on my lap to look. I rub his head and wonder what he'll remember thirty Thanksgivings from now.

We take our son Spencer camping. It is the summer of his second year. Next to the bathhouse, there's a yellow slide that he's forever climbing up and gliding down. I wonder if he'll remember how I caught him at the bottom and whirled him in the air. How once I missed and he tumbled in the dust. How that night he fell asleep on Mommy's lap by the campfire and woke up in the morning sticky with marshmallow.

Sometimes I make the mistake of needing everything to be a memory, of straining to make every moment a snapshot. Going through life with a camera to the eye, wanting the world to fall in step with my expectations. I forget that along with the marshmallows come the mosquitoes, and that no amount of wishing otherwise changes that. Life isn't only about the "should be," the moments gone but treasured; it's also about the "is," the tumbles and the bugs.

I live in this struggle between myth and reality, between "should be" and "is." Went camping once with a friend and tried to pitch my tent on granite ground. Spent a half hour pounding in plastic stakes. My friend said, "Phil, sometimes you just have to pitch your tent somewhere else." This we call flexibility; if we're blessed, we learn it early. If we don't, life is immeasurably more difficult than it needs to be.

This is the blessing of children. For all the difficulties they bring us, they bring their gifts, too. I've learned more patience in two years with my son than in thirty years on my own.

Spencer, my son, cures me of my fevered pounding; this sturdy boy-man so unversed in "oughts" and "shoulds." In truth, he is the resident Wizard of Is, giving me a heart for life on reality's road. Life on this road is life in the slow lane, a pace beyond my fevered pounding.

From my little wizard I learn to live the "is" and leave the "should be" to God.

Hearth and Home

I have a friend who's all the time gone. Canada one month, Florida the next. Always talking about where he's been and where he's headed. He's a fine man, though he makes me wonder why staying home has such low appeal.

I'm a confirmed homebody. When I'm gone, I call home twice a day to stay abreast of things. Florida is fine, but home is better. Home is where my children are. It's where I planted the ivy that's next to the lilac bush that's next to the porch swing. Which is were we sit in the evening when the shadows are long.

Home is where my wife is, who gets up a half-hour before I do to make breakfast. Not because she's my wife and has to, but because she's a loving person and she wants to.

Home is where I watch my boys every afternoon when my wife goes off to work to analyze systems, a distinctly twentieth century job I know nothing about. Home is where I put my boys down for a nap, while I clean up the lunch dishes. It's where my sons build Lego castles and gather pine cones.

Home is where I've learned patience, what little I have. And love. And just about everything else worth knowing. I've included a few stories about my church family, too. Quakers don't ordinarily use the terms "brother" and "sister," though if we did, these would be the folks I'd have in mind.

Why My Wife
Bought Handcuffs

When I was twenty-three years old, I made the best decision of my life. I asked a beautiful, witty woman to be my wife, and she accepted, against the advice of her friends, her family, and a goodly portion of the Western world. On our wedding day, the bridesmaids wore black.

For eight years, I was the model of responsibility. I worked hard. I dried the dishes. I lowered the toilet seat. Then my wife became pregnant. I attended birthing classes and learned to commiserate. When we brought Spencer home, I rose with her to feed him. And when he regurgitated on me, I bore it with good humor.

Three months after his birth, Joan returned to part-time work. On the morning of her departure, she cautioned me to keep a close eye on our son. My feelings were hurt, and I said as much.

"Please, honey, haven't I proven myself reliable?" Thus, I can only think it was the pain of mistrust which caused me to forget my son when I went to the grocery store that afternoon.

I was on my way there and turned around to see him. He was missing! I raced home and found him in his crib, glowering, and I knew what he was going to say when he learned to talk. So I confessed to Joan myself, over a candle-lit dinner and a new silver bracelet.

Being a Christian woman, Joan forgave me and offered me another chance. And the very next morning, after she handcuffed Spencer to me, she said, "Honey, I trust you."

Reflection on this experience has taught me two things: First, having children causes irreparable damage to those areas of the brain having to do with memory; and second, uh, what's the second point? Oh, yeah, the second point is this: We all feel forgotten sometimes.

Actually, I'd learned that second lesson at an early age. My family drove off and forgot me once, too. We were on vacation—five kids, Mom, and Dad—and stopped to eat at a Stuckey's. I was in the bathroom when they climbed back in the car and headed out. They went twenty miles before discovering they were short a kid. Took a quick vote and decided to come back for me. It was almost a tie, but at the last minute Mom changed her mind.

So sometimes each of us feels forgotten. Saddest line in the Bible is when Christ asks God why he forsook him. If Christ felt left behind, how then can we avoid feeling forgotten and forsaken?

Some Bible scholars say that isn't what Jesus meant when he cried from the cross. They say he was quoting the first line of Psalm 22, because to quote the first line was to affirm that psalm's victorious conclusion. I have a great deal of respect for Bible scholars, but they're full of baloney on this one. I think Jesus felt forgotten.

However, the empty tomb tells us he was remembered. And so are we all, which is what I'm going to tell my son, just as soon as I remember where I left him.

Family Vacations

When our son Spencer was six weeks old, I said to my wife, "It's time for a vacation."

"Not a good idea," she cautioned. But she went along because she believes in letting me learn from my mistakes.

We went to a lodge four hours away. Spencer slept the whole way there. I was gloating. Checked in. Went to our room. I was gloating some more. Having kids is a breeze. Mothers are such alarmists.

Then Spencer woke up.

In the book of Revelation, John writes about the seven plagues of divine wrath, ranging from bodily sores to earthquakes. John missed a plague: crying kids. Spencer stopped crying long enough for us to eat dinner. Grandmother-types looked at us and smiled. Before I had a child, I thought they smiled because they liked children. I now understand that they smile because their children are grown.

We went back to our room and went to bed.

Spencer cried all night. The next morning at breakfast we tried to slip out of the restaurant without him, but the manager blocked our escape. Mary and Joseph once left Jesus behind when they were on an out-of-town trip, too. Kind of makes you wonder, doesn't it?

What happened on the way home can only be attributed to sleep deprivation. In an effort to salvage our first family vacation, I drove home on a designated scenic route. The state calls them "scenic routes" because it can't squeeze "twisty-road-that-adds-three-hours-to-your-trip-and-makes-your-kid-carsick route" on one sign.

The next year at vacation time, having forgotten our previous vacation, we drove to a lodge eight hours away. Spencer didn't cry once. He slept soundlessly every night. He rode in his car seat without complaint. We didn't hear a peep from him, but then earplugs have that effect.

That family vacations don't turn out as we'd hoped can only be blamed on television and its inaccurate portrayal of family life. I remember a *Brady Bunch* episode when the Bradys traveled for an entire week without once having to stop to use the bathroom. Florence Henderson sang across three states without anyone pushing her out the car door. When I was growing up, we wouldn't be out the driveway before my brother Glenn had slugged me for breathing on him.

We do ourselves a disfavor when we expect family life to be *The Brady Bunch* revisited. Truth is, most of our families lurch from one mess to another. And that's not an altogether bad thing. Otherwise, how would we cultivate the fine art of forgiveness?

My wife even forgave me after our first vacation. She said at the time, "You can't help it. You come from a long line of men who don't listen to their wives."

I said, "Excuse me, what did you say?"

We're saving up for our next vacation. We're thinking about the mountains.

"There are all kinds of places to lose a kid there," I told my wife.

But she knows I'm just kidding. Actually, I thank God every day for my children. Every day—just some days more than others.

A Family Tradition

My mother was the first to notice how our son Spencer's feet and nose pointed in different directions when he walked. We took him to the bone doctor, who laid our one-year-old on a table and looked him over.

"Your son has turned-in feet and a hernia," he informed us. "The feet we can fix with arch supports, but he'll need an operation for the hernia."

Surgery was scheduled for the following day. I called Mom to tell her the news. She reminded me that hernias were a family tradition. My younger brother David had one when we were little and shared a bedroom. I remembered.

Mom and Dad had called the kids together. "David will need an operation," they told us.

"Could it kill him?" my sister asked.

"We never know," Dad said, "so we'd better pray."

I prayed, but not too hard, since I'd always wanted a bedroom of my own.

David not only survived, he came home from the hospital with the neatest toys. His was the perfect childhood illness—serious enough to merit presents, but not so painful he couldn't play with them.

On the day of Spencer's surgery, my Dad met us at the hospital. I'd "guilted" him into it. Fifteen years before, he'd skipped my high school graduation—sitting in a boiling gym while a local pundit admonished the students to rise above their mediocrity not being his idea of a good time. So he stayed home. Now he feels guilty about it and pretty much does whatever I ask, especially if I start humming "Pomp and Circumstance." So I called him and pointed out that my therapist feels very positive about my chances for a complete recovery barring any further rejection and, sure enough, Dad was at the hospital bright and early.

Everything came out fine. The arch supports did the trick, and the half-hour surgery was textbook. Even the scars went away. Blessed is the family whose gravest problems are so easily remedied.

A cousin of mine gave birth some years ago. A long-faced doctor came out and told her that her son had three holes in his heart. It tore a hole in her heart, too. Some scars are a long time healing.

One thing I've never understood is why I'm so blessed—good parents, good wife, good kids, good job—and others aren't. I used to think it was because I was nice to God, until I met some battered saints. Now I just think there's a randomness in this world beyond my understanding. The apostle Paul said that on this side of things we see in a mirror dimly.

If you woke up this morning and your kids were healthy and your parents loved you, then you don't have any problems. You might think you do, but you don't. And if at night, when you steal into your child's room and watch her little body rise and fall with the breathing, and your heart aches with love, consider your life sublime.

"Patches"

Spencer was a year old when Joan and I took him for his first haircut. We wanted to take him to Linda, our beautician friend, but she won't work on toddlers. Had we been smart, we'd have asked why. Instead, we took him to a barbershop around the corner. The proprietor, Ed, didn't ask our preferred style. Just got out the clippers, went to work, and nine bucks later we were calling our son Patches.

On the drive home I did a little math. Nine bucks a month for eighteen years equals nearly two thousand dollars. Two thousand dollars for the privilege of calling our son Patches. At this point, a reasonable man would have gone back to his beautician friend and asked, "Now why is it you don't cut children's hair?" Instead, with confidence brimming over, I said to Joan, "I've been to college. I can cut my son's hair." I later learned that college has nothing to do with cutting hair. Indeed, a few more years of education might have caused me to reconsider the task I was about to undertake.

Joan, Patches, and I were at the department store the following weekend and came across a haircutting kit on sale! As a student of theology, I perceived this to be a sign from God. Joan had her doubts and put forth a vigorous argument. "A haircut was Samson's ruination," she warned me.

"Samson was a free-love hippie," I rejoined. "Besides, the apostle Paul said that men with long hair will burn in Hades." He didn't really say that, but I knew she wouldn't know that.

During the following weeks, I observed my son closely for evidence of hair growth. The evening before my debut as hair designer, I sharpened and oiled the clippers, then retired early to gain sufficient rest.

What happened the next day was *Father Knows Best* meets *Apocalypse Now*. Because Joan had forbidden me to strap Spencer in his chair, I could hardly be blamed for the catastrophe that followed. Actually, things were going fine until I turned on the clippers. Then Spencer jumped, and the clippers took on a mind of their own. By the time I turned them off, his head had been clear-cut. The good news in all of this was discovering that a baseball cap is even cheaper than a haircutting kit.

The thing I admire most about my wife, other than her movie-star looks and Mother Teresa saintliness (can you tell she's still mad at me?), is her uncanny knack of knowing what she's good at and what she isn't. All too often I end up spinning my wheels in fields I should have steered clear of in the first place.

The apostle Paul knew this. He not only talked about hair, he also mentioned something about valuing your gifts and working from your strengths. Which I suspect was what my wife was trying to tell me when she hid my clippers.

Right Hearts

There were five children in my family when I was growing up—four sons and one daughter. My sister, Chick, was the oldest child, and I came in at number four. Occasionally she would baby-sit us and, though we were bigger, she had a strong right hook and thus our wary respect. She was the scout for the family wagon train, and the rest of us looked to her to show us the way.

Most of the family "firsts" belong to Chick except for marriage. She and Tom got a late start on their nuptials and wanted to squeeze in three children before she turned forty. They had three boys in three years, which is not the textbook way to go about it.

There have been some problems, mostly with their oldest boy, the three-year-old, who acquired the habit of locking his two younger brothers in their bedrooms. Been a lot of anxious moments spent jimmying open door locks while those toddlers were on the other side of the door stuffing who knows what in their mouths, choking, and turning blue.

Tom and Chick took all the doorknobs off, except for the one on their bedroom door, which they turned around so that the lock was on the outside of the room. This worked fine until one morning when my sister was making her bed and heard the door shut behind her with her oldest boy inside her room and the door locked behind him from the outside. The other children were downstairs, unsupervised and inaccessible, probably at that very moment poking their tongues into electrical sockets.

She sat on the bed and cried and cried and cried. Forty years old, three children, and she's headed for nervous breakdown country. This beautiful woman who graduated from college with a perfect 4.0, outwitted by a three-year-old. At that moment, she believed in day care as never before.

She stuck her head out the window and yelled for a neighbor to come over and unlock her bedroom door, which a neighbor did. Chick was humiliated. She called me that night to tell me about it. She asked me not to tell anyone. I told her not to worry, her secret was safe with me.

She said, "Why did we turn that lock around? What were we thinking?"

I admired her candor. If that had been me, I don't think I would have told anyone, or if I had, I would have found a way to make it someone else's fault. I have this sad little habit of needing others to think well of me. Not my sister. She was candid and willing to admit her lapse. Such a refreshing change from our know-it-all tendencies.

I was singing in an Easter choir once, and a man asked me why the song said Jesus died on a tree. I was so eager to impress, I gave him a long, seminary-type answer about crucifixion methods in first-century Palestine. He listened to me go on, then said, "Oh, I just thought maybe they used the word 'tree' because it rhymed."

A lot of folks think closeness to God means knowing all the right answers. But I don't agree. I think closeness to God begins the night we toss and turn in bed, realizing we don't know it all. Look at the Bible. Some of its finest saints were long on questions: Job on his ash heap, the disciples asking Jesus to teach them to pray, Nicodemus grilling Jesus late into the night, even Jesus on the cross.

Having spent much of my life showing off my smarts, I nearly choke on the words "I don't know." Still, I suspect those words might be the kingdom keys. What it boils down to is that God doesn't care whether or not we have right answers. Just right hearts.

Surprise, Surprise, Surprise!

My wife and I waited eight years to have children. I was in college, then graduate school, and thought I was too busy. My mother had five children in seven years, was principal of a school, and attended college all at the same time. And she did a good job, which I point out to her every Saturday when I visit her at the Home for the Mentally Distraught.

Despite our childless state, my wife and I were willing, indeed eager, to share our perspective on child-rearing with anyone who would listen. Now that we have children, we seldom offer advice. The moment you tell someone else how to raise their kid, the odds increase that your own child will turn up on *America's Most Wanted*.

So we don't give advice anymore, because as parents we've realized we don't know anything about children. Before we had children, we knew everything. Now we have children, and the only parent we feel superior to is Ma Barker.

It's been hard to admit my ignorance about child-rearing. It's easy to be smug when you're driving home from someone else's house saying, "When I have children, they will never act like that." Now when our childless friends visit, I tell them when they leave, "Don't talk about us on your way home." They know what I mean.

Most experiences don't turn out the way we'd planned. Parenting is one of them.

Take Spencer's second Christmas. Someone in the church gave him a Nativity set as a gift. He was particularly taken with the wise men, one of whom he used as tableware. Dipped Balthasar up to his ears in ketchup and licked him clean. My wife said, "Honey, don't dip the wise man in the ketchup."

There are many things we anticipated telling our children. Things like, "Because I said so, that's why!" and "Not in this house you won't!" and even "Don't put that in the toilet!" But we never imagined ourselves saying, "Don't dip the wise man in the ketchup!"

That's the kick about life. We think we have it figured out, but then we wade in and discover otherwise. Kind of like Gomer Pyle used to say, "Surprise, surprise, surprise!"

All in all, this is a good thing. For when our

future is sure and certain, when all the corners are tucked in nice and neat, there is no need for faith.

Consider King David. He grew up a shepherd, which was nothing to write home about. If your job can be done by a dog, it's time to worry. So David grew up a shepherd, but he died a king. Goes to show we never know what direction life will take.

This is especially true of being a parent. We never know everything there is to know. Only solution is doing your best and trusting God for the rest. At least that's what my sainted mother used to tell me, back in my younger days, when I knew it all.

Handyman Blues

When we had our first child, everyone said we'd have to build on. Our house had three bedrooms and a good-sized living room, so I couldn't figure out why we needed more room. Plus, in Russia they cram twenty people into a two-room apartment. Then our son turned two, and I learned what every parent knows: The extra space isn't for the kids; it's for the parents.

We decided to convert our basement into living space. Called in a contractor for an estimate. Made sure to tell him about needing access to the pipes, because every now and then a big gob of potato peels jams the garbage disposal, so I have to go down to the basement, open up the pipe, and ram a clothes hanger through to loosen things up.

First, we had to get the basement dry. Lately, it's been getting wet every time it rains. I figured the drainage tile coming off the rain gutters was clogged with roots from our maple tree, which I will cut down just as soon as I get my chain saw fixed. (I broke it trying to cut some bricks.) Turned out it wasn't roots. It was a squirrel that had fallen in the down spout and got stuck. Basically, what I had was a squirrel cork. I rented a plumber's snake—twenty-five feet of cable with a slicer/dicer on the end, and now my basement is Sahara dry.

Before they drywalled the basement, I was told I'd have to clean the mildew off the walls. This was something I didn't understand. I was drywalling to hide the mildew, so first I had to clean the mildew? Why bother drywalling?

I forgot to tell the contractor that sometimes the dirty water from the washing machine backs up through the floor drain. But I stuck a wad of duct tape in the drain and took care of that little problem.

I have a friend who took a class in home maintenance. His house is perfect. When he needs a screwdriver, he goes right to his workshop and gets it. When I need a screwdriver, I head to the kitchen for a butter knife. I hate it when he comes to my house. He says things like, "I'm not trying to alarm you, but the electrical outlets probably shouldn't throw out flames when you turn on a lamp."

I have another friend who hires everything done. He's a man who's made his peace with his ineptitude. Not me. I come from the school of rugged individualists. I figure Daniel Boone never called a plumber.

Sometimes my three-year-old wants to help with household repairs. Once we fixed a leaky faucet together. I forgot to turn off the water before I started, and a geyser hit the kitchen ceiling. The next time we fixed a faucet, he put on his raincoat. Quick learner, my son.

Tradition has it that Jesus was a carpenter. That means he went into people's homes to fix things. You'll note he found another line of work pretty quickly. Wise man, our Savior.

Advice Givers

If a well-intentioned person says to you, "Now it's none of my business, but if that were my child, I would...," please, for the sake of our Lord, stifle your impulse to choke them.

Before our first child was born, my wife and I read several books about parenting. When Spencer arrived, we discovered just how useful those books can be, particularly for chewing on.

When our second son, Sam, was born, my mother came to help. She's a smart woman who reads quite a bit. She had just read a book about parenting and was eager to share her knowledge. Spencer, then two years old, threw a tantrum while Mom was with us. I hadn't slept for two days, and after an hour of crying—mine, not his—I gave Spencer what he wanted.

"Boy, that was a mistake," Mom warned. And she proceeded to tell me that if Spencer gets what he wants by throwing a fit, there's no telling where he'll end up.

"Probably in Congress," I told her.

Mom even had advice about sleeping. She advised us to have baby Sam lie on his back to prevent crib death. But someone else said they should lie on their stomachs for the same reason. So to be safe, I built a rotisserie crib.

Be sure to pray that your child escapes the usual infant ailments, because giving up vacation time to watch your kid is a real drag. But also because advice givers come out of the woodwork when they catch a whiff of sickness. Surprisingly, many people spoke about the curative power of whiskey in small doses. So I tried it, but it only made me lightheaded and woozy.

The worst advice we received was from a man who told us that holding our baby would spoil him. Obviously, he didn't understand how babies require the intimacy that cuddling provides. Besides, cuddling babies is fun and almost makes up for what our children do to us as teenagers.

The best advice we received was from the lady who told us about baby-sitters.

The Bible offers parenting advice. It speaks of sparing the rod and spoiling the child. Some folks think this means spanking your child, but the psalmist speaks of a rod which gives comfort. "Thy rod and thy staff they comfort me." So it really has more to do with gentle guidance.

I believe I've got this advice thing figured out. It isn't that we think we know more than the parents. It's mostly about lending a hand with something as neat as raising a child. It's the same principle behind planting a tree. Twenty years later, we come upon it and delight that we had a part in its growing.

So when folks start telling you how to raise your child, don't think of them as busybodies, but as tree planters. That way, if your little sapling goes bad, you'll have someone else to blame.

The Second Child

When we were expecting our first child, we decided we wanted to have five children. Then our first child was born, and we thought two children had a nice ring to it. We were at the grocery store when we decided that. Figured if God had wanted us to have more than two children, he'd have made bigger shopping carts.

Then we became pregnant with our second child. A friend told us that second pregnancies weren't nearly as exciting as first pregnancies. We thought she was terrible for saying that, but after a while we noticed she was right. When our first pregnancy test came up positive, I called a hundred of my closest friends. When our second pregnancy test turned pink, I called my therapist.

Then our second son, Sam, was born. At this writing he is three months old. When our first son was three months old, we added a room to house his photograph collection. After three months, son number two has one of those goofy hospital pictures, which looks suspiciously like the goofy hospital picture of our first son, which makes me think it really isn't him. Somewhere there's a factory cranking out a dozen different goofy baby pictures, and the nurse just hands you one that resembles your kid.

Then there's the matter of clothing. First children have a wardrobe that would put Elizabeth Taylor to shame; second children take after Jed Clampett. You even catch yourself treating the children differently. First babies you treat like porcelain, second babies like Tupperware. Once heard Bruce Lansky say that when his first child dropped his pacifier, they boiled it for ten minutes. When his second child dropped her pacifier, they told the dog to fetch.

Even our friends treat our second child differently. When our first son was born, thirty-five people came to visit us in the hospital. When child number two was born, we got one visitor, but it was a mistake. Turns out she was looking for the folks in the next room over who were having their first child.

I myself am a fourth child. Took my dad eighteen years to learn my name. Grew up thinking my name was "Glenn...I mean, Doug... I mean, David...I mean, Phil...." But I don't mind being a fourth child. Truth is, I kind of like it. Gave my parents the chance to test their theories on my brothers and sister. I like to think of them as rough drafts.

Lots of stories in the Bible about siblings. In the Old Testament, the firstborn son inherited the whole shebang. In the New Testament, the story changes. The Gospel of Luke tells of a certain man who had two sons. Turns out it was the second who got the fatted calf. Probably to make up for the hand-me-downs.

One thing I've noticed. When I pray for my children at night, my affection for each is the same. I suspect that's how God must feel too. For him, every child is a firstborn. As the old song says, "Jesus loves the little children...." Even the second ones.

Presents and Presence

When Joan and I were expecting our first child, we received the usual warnings regarding lack of sleep, dirty diapers, and temper tantrums. Still, we looked forward to being parents. That's because no one told us about birthday parties.

When our oldest son neared age three, we mistakenly asked him what he wanted for his birthday. At first, all he wanted was a tricycle. We thought that was cute, so we made a big deal out of it. Thus encouraged, he asked for the entire toy department at Wal-Mart. A friend of ours with four kids laughed when we told her about this. She said our first mistake was telling him he had a birthday.

One of my friends has a daughter a few months older than our son, which is the worst possible thing that could have happened because they give great parties for their child, which gets ours pumped up for his. When their daughter turned three, they actually rented a pony for her birthday party. The rest of us were livid, because now we would have to hire a pony for our kids. Thank God, the pony went nuts and bucked a kid off, so my son doesn't want anything to do with ponies. I guess it's true that all things work together for good for those who love the Lord.

Then there's always the little matter of whom to invite to your children's birthday parties. We invite a lot of people, for two reasons. First, the more stuff our kids get from other people, the less we have to buy. Second, a lot of people have made us mad, and this is a good way to pay them back. Like our "friend" who faked a Mexican accent and said, "Sorry, no speaka English," when we were calling around looking for a baby-sitter.

I know a guy who's a Jehovah's Witness. They don't celebrate birthday parties. When I asked him why, he said it's because the only birthday party in the Bible cost John the Baptist his head. And here I am moaning that my son's birthday cost me an arm and a leg.

One birthday our oldest boy got so many toys he sat in the living room and cried. All those options overwhelmed him. I know how he felt. I feel that way whenever *The Andy Griffith Show* and *Murder, She Wrote* are on at the same time.

When I was growing up, I never had a big birthday party. There were five children in my family, and Mom and Dad couldn't afford the extravagance. Mom tried to make things special by letting the birthday child decide what we'd have for dinner. We thought that was a treat! Now my wife and I are so tired of deciding what to have for supper, we'd eat monkey tongues if someone showed up to cook them.

You probably won't like my saying this, but I've noticed a correlation between the size of birthday parties and parental employment. If both parents work, a kid can pretty well count on having a big party. I think parents do that to make up for being gone so much. Call me crazy, but I believe children need our presence more than they need our presents.

I've forgotten almost every present my parents ever gave me. But I'll never forget that when I turned twelve my dad took me canoeing for an entire day. So there are presents and there is presence. Blessed are those parents who learn the finer gift early on.

My Cup Runneth Over, and So does My Toilet

My sons buy me cards every year at Father's Day. I pay for them, but it's the thought that counts. One year, my card had a star on it. It was actually a bar mitzvah card, but my two-year old likes stars, so that's the card I got to open at the breakfast table.

We went over to my father's house that afternoon. Most everyone in the family was there because in my family, if you don't show up, you become the topic of conversation. My second cousin wasn't there, so we talked about him. He's a fairly young man but is retired because he's filthy rich. We were glad he wasn't there, since we've been wanting to talk about him for a long time.

None of us like him because he's not only rich, he's happy. We come from a long line of poor people who've been able to endure poverty by believing that rich people are unhappy so a person is better off poor. But my cousin has gone and shattered that myth. He is rich and happy, which makes the rest of us miserable.

We talked about his house. He is married and has no children, but his home has five bathrooms. My grandpa was betting the toilet paper bill alone would break him. I can't imagine having five bathrooms. Our house has one and a half bathrooms, and just keeping those going can be burdensome.

Like the week after Father's Day, when my wife walked into the bathroom and noticed the carpet was damp, and I told her not to worry because it was just humidity. But the next day, the water was squishing up in between our toes. It was less like humidity and more like an underground spring.

Then I noticed that whenever we flushed, water ran down the back of the tank. I'd never worked on toilets before, but I thought it would build my character, which is what people say when they're too cheap to call a plumber. I worked on it for a few hours before stopping to take a nap. Which is when my wife called a plumber who came and fixed it in five minutes in exchange for the title to our house.

The only comfort I took in all of this was knowing that my cousin has five toilets to take care of, which I think is God's way of teaching him that wealth has its disadvantages.

Wealth does have its disadvantages. Not that I would know this personally, but I suspect when you're rich you're always wondering why people invite you to parties. Do they like you, or do they like your money? I never wonder why people invite me to parties. It's because they like my wife.

There's a story in the New Testament about a rich man. One day, he asked Jesus what it took to inherit eternal life. Jesus told him to keep the commandments, and when the rich man said he'd done that, Jesus told him to sell all he had and give the money to the poor. And the guy stood around waiting for the punch line. Except Jesus wasn't kidding. The Bible says the man walked away sad, for he was very rich. Personally, I don't think he was rich. I think he was the poorest of the poor.

Let's talk about rich. Every year at Father's Day, I get bar mitzvah cards. I love my wife, and she loves me. Got so many friends our house can't hold them, an icebox full of food, and two toilets. How's that for wealth?

My toilet may runneth over, but so does my cup.

Guys

When I was six years old, my parents gave me a rifle for Christmas. It was a pop gun, which they considered harmless, which is why they bought it for me. What they hadn't counted on was a boy's capacity to turn even the most innocuous object into an instrument of violence. While it was true that the gun couldn't fire a bullet, it did make one heck of a club, which I learned while engaging my brother in hand-to-hand combat.

Shortly after that, my mother grew concerned about war toys and wouldn't buy us any more guns. That was fine with us, since by then we had discovered football. Mr. Smitherman was my football coach. I don't remember much about him, except that he was always yelling at us to kill the other team. That was on Saturdays. On Sundays he taught Sunday school, mostly stuff from the Old Testament about God smiting people.

All of this was done, of course, to prepare us

guys for the "real" world, which would chew us up and spit us out if we weren't tough. What it actually did was turn us into insensitive brutes whose idea of entertainment was making body noises with our armpits.

Then it came time for us to date, and we had to be sensitive, which to us meant not laughing out loud at Barry Manilow songs.

Then we went away to college and began bathing regularly, which helped us persuade delicate young ladies to become our brides. So we got married and went back to being slobs.

But then we had children. And one Saturday morning, our wives woke up, gave us the these-are-your-kids-too look and said, "I'm going out today, so you'll need to watch the kids." Which meant we had to be—arrggh! I hate this word—nurturing.

Yes, that's right, we had to be nurturing, which meant we had to sing nursery songs to our children. This is harder than it sounds. Mothers can do this because they have a nursery song gene. Even though we guys are at a disadvantage in this department, I was pleased to see my sons respond favorably to Conway Twitty. Then the unthinkable happened. My wife wanted to start working outside the home every afternoon. And she wanted me to stay home with the kids. This was not in our marriage contract, but I couldn't get out of it because the alternative would have meant working.

So now I stay home almost every afternoon with my sons. At first, I found it embarrassing when I had to explain to another guy that I couldn't do something because I had to watch my sons. So I'd say things like "Can't meet you then; my boys and I are going to work on the car that afternoon." So what if it was a Lego car?

Then the oddest thing happened: I caught myself enjoying it. When I realized this, I was holding Sam on my lap, and he smiled his ten-week smile at me, and I thought how that beat any moment I'd ever spent on the golf course.

I knew if I stayed a Christian this would happen—that one day tenderness would win out. Some of the guys don't understand this, but I don't much care. I still don't tell them I have to watch my sons. Now I tell them I get to, as if it's a special treat. And it is.

Family Life and Other Reasons Jesus Never Married

Several years ago, my aunts made their annual spring visit to my folks' house. We were sitting on the front porch when they mentioned how nice it would be to have a family reunion before my grandmother went to glory. I looked at Dad. I could tell he wasn't wild about the idea because he was sticking his finger down his throat and making a gagging sound. But they applied a little sisterly pressure, and within a week invitations were speeding to the hinterlands.

The reunion was held a few months later. We had more than a hundred people there, including my grandmother, who was so close to meeting her Maker that some of my family were telling her what they wanted when she died.

Everybody was saying how nice it was that she got to see all the family before she passed. But I'm not so sure it was all that great a comfort. You see, my grandmother was a dignified lady. Lived a good deal of her life in England.

Afternoon-tea-with-pinky-finger-out kind of lady. So I don't think she was particularly soothed when my third cousins played "Dueling Banjos" on their armpits.

My second cousin was a school superintendent before he retired. He's kind of the family hero. Everybody has a lot of respect for him. A very thoughtful man, filled with wisdom and sound judgment, which he demonstrated by staying home.

I have another cousin who has a doctorate. He lives in Chicago and does research for a university. He goes to South America a lot, but I'm not sure why. Truthfully, I don't think he's a real doctor because when I asked him to play golf he didn't know how.

My godfather was there. He's the richest person in our family and also an atheist, which I didn't think godparents were allowed to be. Funny thing is, none of us knows how he got his money. One of my relatives thinks he sells drugs. Someone else mentioned that he sells insurance, though that's hardly an improvement.

Then there's my grandfather. He's not on my dad's side of the family, but since he lives nearby, he came just the same. He was originally from Belgium but sailed to America when he was a boy. When he was a young man, he dated Gene Hackman's mother, which means Gene Hackman could have been my father if Grandpa had married her. That means I'd have ended up in Hollywood kissing starlets, which would have cost me my job as a Quaker pastor and gotten me in trouble with my wife. So I guess it all worked out for the best.

I don't know if Jesus ever attended a family reunion. The Bible mentions that he once went to a wedding. His mother was there, too, so it was probably a family affair. They ran out of drinks halfway through the reception, so Jesus took some water and turned it into wine. Except in the Baptist Bible, where he turned it into grape juice.

Jesus said some confusing things about family life. On the one hand, he told us to love one another. But another time, at least according to Luke, Jesus said no one could be his disciple unless he hated his family. Perhaps that was Jesus' way of saying that we're to put him before everyone else. Or maybe he had just heard his third cousin play "Dueling Banjos" with his armpit and he meant it literally.

Who knows what Jesus meant by that? I do know this, though. The more I work on loving

Jesus, the easier it becomes to love my family. Maybe it's really a matter of putting first things first. When we love the way of Jesus first, we're then sufficiently equipped to love our family. Even third cousins with talent galore.

Confessions

$\mathcal{I}$ grew up Roman Catholic at Saint Mary's Church in Danville. Father McLaughlin was the first pastor I remember. He was hard of hearing, so when we confessed our sins, we had to shout them out loud for the good father to hear. It was in this way that I was introduced to human depravity—sitting in the back pew overhearing admissions of sin and vice.

My first confession took place when I was seven years old. I couldn't think of anything to confess, ignorance of personal sin and shortcoming being one of my youthful peculiarities. Not wanting to disappoint Father McLaughlin, who seemed so eager to confer forgiveness, I made up sins to confess. The first week I confessed to calling my sister a dirty name, though I really hadn't, for to have done so would have assured my slow and painful death. The next week I confessed to disobeying my parents, which again was absurd, for disobedience was simply not allowed in our home. By the third week, it occurred to me that I could truthfully confess to lying, and I went to confession pleased that I would finally know the exquisite pleasure of authentic sin confessed.

Father McLaughlin listened to my admission of sin and assigned a penance: three "Our Fathers"; three "Hail Marys"; then go to the person to whom I had lied, admit my untruth, and ask for forgiveness. The first two were easy, but since he was the one to whom I had lied, the third piece was a bit tricky. I wasn't sure what the penalty was for lying to a priest, but I knew it had to be stiff. Would I have to go to the Pope's office? I had seen the Pope's picture hanging in our church, and he looked like a school principal, stern and forbidding. It was this dilemma that first turned my eyes toward the Quakers, a people in our town known for their tendency to go easy on spiritual renegades like myself.

My record of confession did not improve when I became a Quaker and was gladdened to learn that public admission of sin was neither expected nor desired. Occasionally an evangelist would visit and describe his life of sin before he met the Lord. We Quakers would grow alarmed, thinking he might invite us to reciprocate. Sin was not something to be confessed, it was something to keep hidden. Why spend a lifetime building a reputation of virtue, only to shoot yourself in the foot with public confession?

This is why I was so startled when a Quaker woman actually rose during our meeting for worship and confessed her sin. She admitted to all types of sordid activity and invited us to pray for her, which we did. Afterward, she appeared refreshed, her public confession a shower for her soul. The rest of us left worship weighed down, as if the tax of her sin were charged to us. This was our fault, not hers, since we were reluctant to let her sin sink in the sea of God's forgetfulness. Instead we kept it afloat by thinking on it time and again. I yearned for my Catholic days when sin confessed was sin forgotten—and forgiven.

We shock so easily. We ogle fallen saints as if sin were truly a rarity, an unusual bird paying us a visit which sends us scurrying to a book to identify such an alien thing. Are TV preachers the only ones who still believe that all have sinned and fallen short of God's glory? In our worship of self-esteem, have we turned a blind eye to sin and consequently to the refreshing touch of divine amnesty?

This I desire: to sit once more on Saint Mary's back pew, overhearing the steady rhythm of sin and grace. Not to gloat, but rather to marvel at a people's confidence in God's sure pardon.

Life's Too Short

I once spent a pleasant evening in the company of friends who thought my father had just passed away. I had gone to a church gathering to hear a friend speak, and people came up to me to ask how I was doing. Not in the usual way we ask people how they're doing, when we're being polite and really don't care to hear, but in a sincere way with their hands on my shoulder and their voices funeral soft.

At first, I thought they were just sucking up to me, since a few weeks before a rumor had circulated that I had come into some money, which wasn't true. I hadn't refuted it, though, because if you're going to have a rumor floating around about you, that's a good one. It sure beats all the other rumors about me, most of which are true.

Then a man sat down beside me, leaned over, and said, "I'm sorry about your father." I had talked with my dad that very afternoon but grew alarmed at the thought that something could have happened to him in the short hours since. It would be like my mother to forget to call me if something had happened. I was sitting there being mad at my mother, when the man said, "I read about it in yesterday's paper." What had happened was that a man with my father's name had died and the survivors included a son with my name.

People from three different churches had prayed for me that morning. If you can ever arrange it to experience that much compassion without having to suffer the pain of a loved one's passing, I encourage you to take full advantage of it. It was a splendid evening.

Oh, there were a few drawbacks. One guy, whom I thought was my friend, didn't say a word to me. The more I think about that, the madder I get. If his father had died, I'd have said something to him. It takes something like this to show you who your real friends are.

The other drawback is having to explain to people that your father is alive and well after they've gone out on an emotional limb to express their sorrow. You can see how they might be embarrassed. It's hard to talk with someone who has experienced a loss, so after you've been a comfort to someone it's natural to feel good about yourself. I hated to deny them that feeling, so after a while I stopped explaining and started thanking them for their kindness. It seemed the nobler gesture. Naturally, I'll have to set the record straight someday, but not until folks have stopped dropping food off at the house.

I called my dad and told him he was supposed to be dead. He thought it was pretty funny and said it explained why people at the grocery store had stared at him that day. My mom didn't laugh and thought we were sick for joking about it. I'd hate to be a mother. They exhaust themselves trying to civilize us, and we repay them by watching *The Three Stooges* and letting our pants ride halfway down our bottoms.

Nevertheless, this whole episode has helped me appreciate compassion and those who show it. I've decided I want to be numbered among them. I've also decided to forgive the friend who made no effort to console me. After all, life's too short. Just ask my dad.

Observations

When I was nine years old, we moved from a ranch house to a rambling, turn-of-the-century house across town. The last thing the movers packed were our bicycles, which meant they were the first to come off the truck. I pedaled mine next door to meet the neighbors, whom I was sure would have a nine-year-old boy just waiting to show me the neighborhood ropes. What I got instead was a Quaker widow named Mrs. Draper. Initially, I felt gypped. But after a while, when she began turning out popcorn balls and cookies, I realized I had hit the mother lode.

Mrs. Draper—we called her Mawga—passed the time sitting on her porch swing telling stories about our town and how it used to be. Mawga told how our house had been built by a Civil War veteran as a gift to his daughter. She still called it the Hollowell house after the people who had lived in it back in the 1930s.

If you listened close to Mawga, you'd pick up an insight or two about right living. Mawga was careful to say that she didn't preach, she made "observations." In that spirit, I offer a few observations. I hope you find them as helpful as I found Mawga's.

The Kitchen Table

My hobby is woodworking and has been for a number of years. My foray into wood began when we needed a kitchen table and my wife suggested I build one. We were low on money, and I was between college and graduate school and had the time. I'd never built anything before, but a kitchen table seemed as good a place to start as any.

My grandfather had a workshop set up in the family barn. I'd go there in the morning, turn on the heater, and walk around sniffing the workshop odors. Grandpa had lubricated the drill press once a month since 1950, and I could smell nearly forty years of oil buildup in the corner where it sat. Over by the table saw I smelled sawdust. After a while I became a sawdust connoisseur and could tell the difference between pine sawdust and cherry sawdust. There are few scents more pleasant. The dog slept in the workshop, and I could smell her, too, wet and stagnant, like the pond used to smell with its August coat of scum.

It took me the month of February to build the table. I could have done it quicker, but being tucked away in the barn while winter blasted away outside was so pleasant it made me want to dwell on that page as long as I could. In March, I took the table outside beneath the trees, next to the crocuses that were pushing up, and sanded it down. Grandpa came by and taught me how to use slivers of glass to plane the joints smooth. That's an old woodworker's trick I never would have picked up on my own.

I spent a week massaging five coats of tung oil into the wood. It takes a long time to get the finish right on a piece of furniture, but you can't hurry it, or the flaws will show, and all your hard work will be for nothing. Woodworking is a good way to learn that doing something worthwhile takes time. It is possible to make a table in a hurry. It is not possible, however, to make a table worth passing on to your grandchildren in a hurry.

My wife and I wrapped the table in blankets, loaded it up in the truck, and carried it home. She gave me a brass plate, engraved with my name and the year, to mount on its underbelly. That's so when my children's children play underneath it they'll be able to see when Grandpa built it.

I wanted to buy chairs to match, but we didn't have the money so we made do. Though every time we'd go into an antique store, we'd keep our eyes peeled. I even thought about making chairs, but building a good chair is extraordinarily difficult and time-consuming. I could build a bad chair in a day. After six years of haunting antique stores, we found four chairs. By then, times were better, and we took them home. Each is as fine a chair as can be had, and I intend to enjoy myriad ears of July sweet corn while sitting in them.

A friend came for dinner not long ago. He asked me where I had bought my table, and I told him I had made it. He wanted me to make him one, but I told him no. A man has to be careful not to let his hobby become his business. He was talking about how his kitchen table is forever falling apart and lamenting the shoddy nature of today's craftsmanship. People slapping things together in five minutes expecting them to last a lifetime.

We got to talking about how that isn't only true about furniture, it's true about life. Folks get discouraged because God doesn't make them saints overnight. They don't understand all the years of God-work that go into making one's life a thing of beauty—a lot of shaping, a lot of smoothing, a lot of finishing. And if we rush the process, the flaws will surely show.

Once a week I rub a coat of lemon oil into my table. It reminds me that my table is never really finished. Kind of like me.

Television

The Smiths lived across from us when I was growing up. They were Pentecostals and believed television rotted the soul. They said it was from the devil. They also held that opinion about Catholics and made every effort to convert us to their way of thinking. Their church was up on Lincoln Street. On Sunday nights, my friends and I would ride our bicycles over, sit underneath the windows, and listen to the goings-on. It didn't sound like anything we were hearing at Saint Mary's Catholic Church. My brother went once, and he came home talking about people dancing in the aisles and men playing guitars. I could see where television would be anticlimactic.

The Smiths were the only family I knew without television until I met my friend Jim. His family's television had broken, and they couldn't afford to replace it. So they threw it away and started saving for a new one. But by the time they'd raised the money, they'd decided not to

waste it on a new television set. I couldn't imagine going without television. I asked him what
they did at night. He said he and his wife read a
lot and their kids played board games. Then
they went to bed at seven o'clock.

Shortly after that, my wife and I read some
articles about how destructive television can be
in the formation of values. We were expecting
our first child and, in a fit of pre-parent concern,
gave our TV away. Then one of our friends
thought we couldn't afford a TV, so he and his
wife gave us one of theirs. That was almost four
years ago. We put it in the closet but take it out
every Sunday night to watch *The Andy Griffith
Show.* The rest of the week we read or go for a
drive in the country or sit outside on the porch
swing and visit while the kids play.

I'm beginning to understand that TV is like a
drug. When we first got rid of ours, I experienced withdrawal symptoms. I was edgy and
crabby and out of sorts. Now I can't stand any
television, except for Andy and Barney and
Opie. Mostly, it strikes me as a bucket of sleaze.

I suspect a lot of folks feel that way. Seems
everywhere you turn somebody is railing against
television—from parents to pastors to politicians. They want Hollywood to clean up its act.

Hollywood says they're just showing it like it is. Meanwhile, violence is spinning out of control, and our schools are graduating kids who can't read a job application, let alone a fine book. A lot of smart people lay this at the feet of television.

This is one problem whose solution is a no-brainer. Stop whining, unplug your television set, and put it in the closet. Take it out once a week to watch Andy or any other program that embraces the values you hold dear.

Folks, no one's holding a gun to our heads. No one's saying, "Watch this, or else." If your kids don't like it, tough. Here's where they start learning they can't have everything they want. And if they keep complaining, hand them a book. If your spouse puts up a fuss, then find something to do together that is more compelling than watching *Roseanne*. That shouldn't be too difficult.

I would ask you to excuse my passion on this subject, though I'm not ashamed of it. A day scarcely passes that I don't come across some sedentary soul whose literary tastes go no further than *TV Guide*. The waste of potential appalls me. The Smiths, bless their Pentecostal hearts, were right. Television does kill our souls. And it's not too good for our brains, either.

Vocation

The first job I ever had was delivering newspapers. I had twenty-six customers, but it took more than two hours to deliver the papers. I was raised to believe that it's polite to inquire after a person's health when you see him. Trouble was, all my customers were elderly. When I asked them how they were feeling, they told me.

I did that for three years, then I quit to mow lawns and do odd jobs. Once, after a snowstorm, I earned twenty dollars shoveling out the widows on our street. I showed the money to my dad, and he made me take it back. He said it wasn't right to take money from widows. I learned from that experience. The next time it snowed, I sent my little brother out to shovel.

When I was sixteen, I went away for the summer to work at a national park. I earned fifty dollars a week, plus room and board. We spent the summer helping to renovate a historical building. I met my first girlfriend there. Ever since then, I've had a weakness for women in hard hats.

Then I came home and got a job working in a grocery store. I used to sack groceries and put canned goods out. I almost went away to college to become a grocery store manager, but my dad advised against it. He said that the hours were long and the pay wasn't all that great. So I became a minister instead. I'm glad my dad was looking out for me.

When I graduated from high school, I worked for an electric utility for five years. I operated big computers. I hated it. To this day, I won't own a computer. People look at me funny when they find out I don't like computers. Once I tried writing on one, and the computer had the gall to suggest that I use one word in place of another. I don't like computers telling me what to do. That's what parents are for.

I quit my computer job, got married, and started college. During college, I had a bunch of different jobs. One summer I got a job with the state highway picking up dead animals along the road. I always mention that in job interviews so prospective employers will know I'm willing to do anything to earn a living.

While I was in college, I was hired by a country church to be their pastor. After worship I would find grocery sacks of sweet corn in my car. Plus, once a month we'd throw a pitch-in dinner. I was there for four years and gained twenty pounds. One year at Christmas they gave me a hand-stitched quilt. I can't imagine a gentler way to initiate a young pastor into ministry than keeping food in his stomach and quilts on his bed.

Now I pastor a church in the city. Been here six years. No quilt yet, but free baby-sitting and tears when we miscarried and people so tender they make Mother Teresa look like a slacker. I hope God keeps me here a long time.

I've met a lot of people in my lifetime, and over the years I've had a lot of people bare their souls to me. Consequently, I've formed a few insights into what constitutes the good life. The first is this: Never ask people how they're doing unless you really want to know. The second is this: Find a vocation that uses your God-given gifts, or you'll be a miserable wretch of a human being.

That's the God's truth. I know a guy who's a janitor. He is thoroughly convinced that God has called him to be a janitor, and he loves it. He doesn't make much money, but he's one of the happiest persons I know. He worked real hard to put his children through college. So they went down to Bloomington to the state college, and now they earn a ton of money, but none of them are as happy as their father. If you have to choose between following money or following your heart, go with your heart.

There are a lot of things that can't be corrected. Squandering your life in a job that shrivels your soul is one of them.

Tasting Tears

When my wife and I first married, we lived upstairs in an old house owned by a mortician who gave us a rent break every time I helped him bury someone. Eventually, they tore the house down, since in America it's easier to throw something away than to fix it.

We moved into an old farmhouse with thousand-dollar heating bills and wraparound porches. The house sat in the middle of five hundred acres of corn and beans. Came with a barn, a chicken coop turned garage, and a smokehouse. Since I don't smoke, we put our bicycles there. The house also came with a whole tribe of barn cats, one of whom slipped through the screen door, unpacked his cat suitcase, and set up housekeeping. We named him Whittier, after the Quaker poet, and trained him to hide every time the landlord came around checking for violations.

Our neighbor had a cat named Cream Rinse. How that name came into being is an entirely different story. Let me just say it made no difference to the cat who, like most cats, didn't come when he was called anyway. The cat I had as a child came when I called it, but only when I ran a can opener at the same time. What's more important to know is that Cream Rinse and Whittier were nearly identical in appearance, except for a small white spot on Whittier's chin.

We didn't have any children at the time and considered Whittier our "baby." So when I was lying in the bathtub one morning and heard my wife wail and gnash her teeth, I knew something had happened to Whittier. Sure enough, there had been a feline-auto encounter of the worst kind on the road in front of our house. Being the one with burial experience, it fell to me to entomb him out back underneath the walnut tree. Except I didn't have a shovel, so I had to borrow our neighbor's at six o'clock in the morning, which woke her up. Being the mother of Cream Rinse, she was most understanding.

Three days later, I was sitting on the porch swing reading "Dear Abby" (Dear Abby, I have neighbors who borrow my lawn tools at all hours of the day. What should I do?), and Whittier jumped on my lap, white spot and all. Resurrection! Hallelujah! Turns out Whittier had gone to visit relations for a few days, and it was Cream Rinse I'd buried. Perhaps you're wondering how I could have made such a mistake. I will simply mention that when dealing with flattened feline, one doesn't look too closely for identifying characteristics.

Now came the hard part. I had to tell my neighbor it was her cat who'd used up his nine lives. And I had to do it without laughing, it being unwise to chuckle when giving death notices. I'd learned that from my old landlord. But certain aspects of this seemed so humorous, a chortle and a titter slipped right out. Which confirmed her suspicion that I was an unfeeling clod.

Turns out Cream Rinse had gotten his name from Saturday night baths. So they had a history, and she had some tears to shed.

Been times I've wondered how others can be so happy when I'm so miserable. Then other times I've wondered how I can smile when other folks are crying buckets. And how little those tears mean to me sometimes.

Of all the traits we need to cultivate, empathy is the toughest. That's when somebody's crying but someone else is tasting tears. Most of us don't taste anyone's tears but our own. And we wonder why our souls dry up.

So today I aspire toward empathy, for tasting tears other than my own. And I'm going to start with my neighbor, whom Jesus commanded me to love, whether she loans me her lawn tools or not.

Liberty

When our friend's children were waist-high and starting peewee league, my wife and I would take the lawn chairs over and watch a little baseball on summer evenings when the shadows were long. Peewee League is serious stuff in our neck of the woods—matching shirts, big wads of bubble gum, and telling the umpire he's blind. And that's just the parents.

Joan and I were watching on Friday night when Robin, a five-year-old girl, stepped up to bat. Three feet tall, fifty pounds, and sun-blond hair. Her father was the home plate umpire that night, it being his turn. He watched as his little girl knocked the dirt from the bottom of her shoes just like the big leaguers. His little girl. Five years ago, he'd carried her home from the hospital in a fuzzy blanket, crazy with love. Now she was pounding home plate and aiming for the outfield. Where had time gone?

Now he was the umpire. Mr. Objective. Mr. I-have-no-children-so-don't-expect-a-favor. I was watching him. Robin had never actually hit the ball; she was always a second or two late. But today was a new day, and who knows what might happen? Her father weakened a bit and whispered encouragement. I saw his lips move. "Come on, honey. You can do it. Keep your eye on the ball. Remember what I taught you."

The pitcher pitched and Robin swung. Wood met leather, a trickle of a hit down the third base line, and Dad went crazy. Forgot all about impartiality. He jumped up and yelled, "Run, honey, run." And Robin ran. She ran like she had never run before, like she had rockets strapped to her shoes. She ran straight over the pitcher's mound to second base. Skipped first base. Forgot all about it.

Sheer bedlam. Robin on second base jumping up and down, high-fiving one and all, basking in joy. Parents on the sidelines were jumping up and down, too, but for reasons other than joy. The adults gathered at home plate for a high-level conference, thumbing through their dogeared rule books. Can't skip first base. Got to be a rule against that somewhere. After a while, Dad walked over to his little slugger and called her out, while the adults contented themselves that justice had prevailed.

In these days of moral cloudiness, we're tempted to think rules will be our salvation. But a stubborn devotion to rules can kill joy in a snap. Like the time when Jesus healed the man on the Sabbath and the Pharisees cried foul.

Saint Augustine once said, "Love God with all your heart, soul, strength, and mind; and love your neighbor as yourself. Then do anything you want." This is liberty exercised within love's boundary. Love God and neighbor, then do anything you want. That gives love and joy all kinds of room to weave their spell.

Irony is, love and rules have the same goal—helping folks get along. Though love does it through the pull of the heart while rules attempt it with the twist of the arm. Don't get me wrong; I'm not an anarchist. Rules have their place on life's roster. I just think love and joy ought to lead the way.

Stuff

My grandpa comes to my house twice a year. I measure his well-being by how long it takes him to walk up the sidewalk. I've lived here six years, and his walk time has doubled. That's not a good sign.

He walks in, sits down, looks around, and says, "I love this house," though he never says why. Is it the furniture? the cream walls? the beige carpet? Who knows? Grandpa certainly isn't saying. But I know how he feels. I love my house too. It's the closets. Our house has lots of closets and two extra rooms we don't use except when we have company, which means we have a lot of space to store our stuff.

I love stuff and have a lot of it, even though I'm a Quaker who believes in living simply. We have two couches, one love seat, and fifteen chairs. Fifteen chairs may seem like a lot of chairs to you, but I sit in most of them once a day, except for the chair in the laundry room, which is covered with dryer lint. One of the chairs in my living room is more than 150 years old. Whenever we have guests, the heaviest person invariably gravitates toward it. I spend the whole visit on the edge of my chair ready to leap forward and catch the person the moment the chair collapses in a heap.

In addition to the fifteen chairs inside, we have a porch swing, three lawn chairs, and two Adirondack chairs outside. That's so whenever I'm watching my wife do yardwork, I'll have a comfortable place to sit.

We have three kitchen tables, four end tables, three coffee tables, two desks, and a typing table we don't use anymore. Plus a typewriter, two word processors, and more than thirty pens and pencils in the drawer to the left of the kitchen sink. On the off chance I'm struck with a thought, I want a writing surface and instrument close at hand. I also have a gardening table in the garage and a workshop table in the basement. Mostly they're covered with half-finished projects that I'm going to wrap up one of these days when I'm not so busy.

I have two bicycles, though I can ride only one at a time. My wife and children have bikes too. Except for Sam, who's only one. He rides with my wife. We all have helmets, which means we need shelves to store them on. I have six sets of shelves—two in the basement and four in the garage. They're full of half-empty paint cans. I have eighteen of those.

We have three sets of dishes, though we use only one. They're made by Corelle. We've used them for twelve years and are sick and tired of them, but they're too nice to throw away. My aunt gave them to us on our wedding day. If I'd known we were going to be stuck with them this long, I wouldn't have sent her a thank-you note.

We have eleven lamps, four flashlights, two camping lanterns, and a kerosene lamp. Of the four flashlights, only one works, but one of my boys hid it, so when I need a flashlight I use our piano lamp and a long extension cord. Plus we have two boxes of candles and a book of matches from a funeral home. I don't think funeral homes ought to give matches away, since most people use them to light cigarettes. It's hard to believe funeral directors care for us as much as they claim to, when they're passing out matchbooks right and left.

The last time I saw my grandpa, he was talking about all the stuff he wants to give me when he dies. I hope he lives a long time, since I'm in no mood to move. As fun as it is to have all my stuff, it's also a real drag. I'm so busy tending my stuff, my soul gets dust-covered. An old gospel hymn calls this being "rich in things and poor in soul."

The solution to this problem isn't to give all our stuff away. Then Grandpa dies, and we're back where we started. What we need to do is figure out why we want stuff to begin with. Mostly it gets down to thinking it will make us happy. Which it does, but only for a while, then we need more stuff.

As I see it, the only way out is death. Or discipleship, which comes from the word "discipline." At least that's what my dictionary says. And I should know, since I have five of them.

Where I Stand

Jay, a friend of mine, once observed that the only thing it takes to make an insane asylum is an empty room and the right people. He said this during a church meeting, which caused the rest of us to wonder what he was implying.

I've always prided myself on my robust mental health. Thirty-four years old and no breakdown, at least not yet. My wife said I came close once. That was the autumn Saturday we went to Nashville—a small town three counties down where God went overboard with fall leaves. Being a place of beauty in a plain-Jane state, Nashville receives more visitors than Disneyland. Still, it's good to go there at least once a year, if only to be reminded why we don't live in Los Angeles.

I suspect it was the car exhaust fumes that disrupted my thought processes and compelled me to take a shortcut to Nashville. We ended up temporarily misplaced in a little town called Pumpkin Center. It had a gas/grocery/video/

Elvis memorabilia store. I went inside to ask directions. This, despite my father's clear teaching never to ask directions from anyone with three first names.

So I asked Billy Bob Clyde how to get to Nashville. "Well, you go over to Cecil Hopper's place and turn right, then you take a left at Skeeter Hodge's farm, then go straight ahead 'til you reach Nashville."

Now I know why older folks stick compasses on their dashboards.

We finally made it to Nashville. Simply climbed a tree and looked for the smog. Got there in time to buy some ice cream and a genuine rubber tomahawk for our then two-year-old, who has since scalped two cats and a Chihuahua.

I saw my grandpa the next day and told him about our trip. He's in the Fellowship of Compass Carriers. Always knows right where he is and right where he's headed.

I used to laugh at him and call him Columbus. "Hey, Columbus, how's life on the Ninja, the Pinto, and the Ave Maria?" He'd give me a blank stare. My grandpa may not know his history, but he never gets lost.

Truth be told, I sometimes envy folks like my

grandpa, folks who have this sixth sense concerning the life-path they need to take. As for me, I spend a lot of time roaming the back roads, never certain what I think about things most folks are clear on.

My grandpa eyeballs his compass, and down the road he goes. No situational ethics for him, by golly. Right is right, wrong is wrong, and let the chips fall where they may. I'm more of a on-the-one-hand-this-but-on-the-other-hand-that kind of guy.

This can cause problems when you're a minister. Folks expect me to know right where I stand, especially in church meetings. I don't know what this presumes about ministers, but I'm not encouraged.

I'll tell you where I stand. I stand for integrity and for erring on the side of grace and for reading to your children. Oh, yeah, and for staying home on Saturdays in the fall.

The Dog
Who Wouldn't Die

The problem with dogs is their poor sense of timing. Take Blue, for instance, who belongs to some friends of mine. They claim Blue is an Australian Blue Heeler, though I have no way of verifying this, since I know no other Australian Blue Heelers. I'm taking my friends' word on this, who have proven to be honest in all other matters. Blue is seven years old, which is young for an Australian Blue Heeler, some of whom live twenty-five years. That's 175 years to you and me. They are the Methusalehs of dogs.

Blue got sick last year. Her stomach began to swell, and my friends thought she was pregnant. This was a reasonable assumption. In addition to their poor sense of timing, dogs have incredibly loose morals and mate rather indiscriminately.

They took Blue to the veterinarian. He told them Blue was very sick and would likely die. Then he treated Blue, charged them a monstrous sum of money, and sent Blue home to die. Of course, my friends were sad and began to pamper Blue. We do have a tendency to spoil loved ones who are sick. Think of the last time you saw a kid with polio get spanked. See what I mean?

But as I said, most dogs have poor timing. This is certainly true of Blue. Six months after her death sentence, Blue lives on. She is the healthiest dying dog I've ever seen. Now, having been spoiled for so long, Blue has lost all sense of discipline. She chews on clothes and gives her owners a sullen look when they tell her to do something. In a word, Blue has overstayed her welcome. She is the mother-in-law who came for a week's visit and stayed a year.

I was talking with my friends about her. They told how they went through the grieving process six months ago when they thought Blue was going to die. Now they are over their grief and wish Blue had the decency to expire. Until she does, their lives are on hold. They can't take a vacation because they'd have to put her in a kennel. If she died in some small cage surrounded by strangers, they'd feel terrible for the rest of their lives. They're in a real fix. This is why dogs are so infuriating. A cat would have the good sense to succumb in a tasteful and timely manner. Dogs are dense and can't take a hint.

Now my friends are upset with Blue. I know how they feel. One of my brothers got sick when I was little. He came close to dying. Then he got better but not before causing us to miss our summer vacation. That made me so mad. If he was going to make us miss our summer vacation, the least he could have done was die. Some people are so insensitive!

The problem here is one of expectation. Blue's refusal to die on schedule reminds us that life and death aren't always predictable. Things don't always turn out as we'd been led to believe. Marriages begun with tender words and long conversations dwindle down to grudging grunts and strained silence. Careers that began at rocket speed sputter to a midlife halt. It's almost enough to make you scared of hoping.

But the reverse is also true. Tragedy can turn to victory with a few short words. Consider Abraham and Sarah. They'd braced themselves for a life without children—no sticky kisses, no one-tooth baby grins, no lap-sitting grand-kids—when God paid them a visit bearing a box of it's-a-boy cigars.

Life in God's reign is kaleidoscopic in nature. We try in vain to picture life's next scene, while grace is at work resetting the stage. Some dogs just won't die, and some barren lives just won't stay that way.

Soul Tending

I read not long ago how gardening has risen in popularity among young American males. The article quoted a sociologist who attributed this to the male's need to nurture. I thought we were doing it to get out of cleaning the house.

I got serious about gardening the summer my first son was born. Somehow the bulb companies found out and began sending me their catalogs. I ordered a few things and once actually got what I ordered: sixty starts of myrtle, which the catalog described as a "robust, breathtaking carpet of emerald beauty." Today I have a beautiful stand of myrtle underneath my maple tree. I found it in the woods when I was throwing away the dead myrtle I'd gotten from the bulb company.

My neighbors like to garden too. They not only have beautiful flower beds, their yards are exquisite. My dandelions blow into their yard, so they've been encouraging me to kill them, but I don't want to. I like to think of my yard as a melting pot. Everything is welcome—all the huddled weeds yearning to breathe free. I consider it a place of sanctuary, a symbol of Christ's welcoming inclusivity. Besides, every fall my neighbors' leaves blow into my yard, and this is my only way to pay them back.

I have two flower beds in my yard. One is in the middle of the backyard. A big sinkhole opened up right before we moved in, and the previous owner brought in a load of sand to fill it up. Which meant I had a giant litter box for all the neighborhood cats. So one day I built a stone border, brought in a load of topsoil, and planted a tree and flowers. Now it's so pretty the cats bring their friends.

My other flower bed is one of those garden-in-a-can things. When I bought it, I had visions of crisp lace curtains blowing in a July breeze and old clay jars filled to overflowing with wildflowers, like you see in the magazines at the checkout counter. The can promised three hundred square feet of "lush, radiant beauty." It said that in big print. What it said in small print was that you have to turn the earth over to a depth of six inches. I borrowed my neighbor's rototiller, since I wasn't about to let my wife do all that work by hand.

The garden didn't do too well the first summer. Then I read an article about how forest fires cause wildflowers to grow real thick, so I set the garden on fire, and a pine tree, and my gardening shed. Now I know what people mean when they say gardening can be expensive.

The second summer the flowers were thick. When they reached their peak, I cut them and brought them inside. Dug the clay jars out of the basement. Opened up the windows so the lace curtains would blow. Woke up the next morning, and those flowers had gone to the great flower bed in the sky—wilted and bent and sticky with death.

Elton Trueblood talked about how we're a cut-flower world. We sever things from their life source and expect them to flourish. And we cut ourselves off from God and are dismayed when our lives wilt and fade. We spend so much time chasing after the baubles of the world, we're bankrupt when it comes to the treasures of the holy. We want joy and beauty, but we want them without having to stay connected to the One who gives them. So we look for them in the world but come up empty-handed and empty-hearted.

If it's lasting beauty we seek, we're simply

going to have to spend as much time tending
our souls as we do tending our yards.

Seeking and Finding

My father is a leader of men. He exudes horse sense. When guidance is needed, my father's telephone rings. So when the Danville Mushroom Hunters Association was looking for leadership, they turned to my father.

"You must be our president, Norm," they said. "Everyone respects you. People turn to you for advice. Besides, you have a key to Lee Comer's cabin, and we were hoping we could go there this weekend."

The nomination was made. The vote taken. Five to zero, a veritable landslide.

They left for the cabin on a Friday night, stopping on the way to purchase a gallon of wine in obedience to Saint Paul's advice to young Timothy. Ordinarily, these are not religious men, except for when it comes to 1 Timothy 5:23; then they are fundamentalists to the core.

Dad woke them up at 4:30 the next morning. Any mushroom hunter worth his salt knows that alone of all the mushroom family, the morel is at its finest in the early morning hours. Once the sun rises, the morel loses its appeal. It's a nocturnal mushroom. When the sun hits a morel, it's done for, but if you pick it while it's still wet with morning dew and get it into briny water within an hour or so, you'll enjoy an unrivaled delicacy. You have to plan accordingly.

The first mistake many mushroom hunters make is their failure to organize. Fortunately, Dad came prepared.

"To begin with, we need a vision statement," he said. "Every organization worth its salt has one. I would like to suggest 'Semper Fidelus' or 'Always Faithful.'" Dad watched a lot of Marine movies. They voted. It was unanimous; not a person disagreed. Mostly because their heads hurt too much from heeding Saint Paul the night before.

After breakfast, they went to the woods. The morel mushroom is one of nature's more elusive quarries. Buckskin-clad men at one with nature have been reduced to tears in their search for this Holy Grail of the mushroom family. Children, however, have been known to stumble upon entire acres of this delicacy only to return as adults and not find even the smallest spore of a morel. The memory of it haunts them in their sleep.

The first day's search proved fruitless, as did the next day's. They went home more or less morel-less. Dad, being a leader of men, called an emergency meeting of the D.M.H.A. that week. He sat at the head of the table pondering their failure. One of the members ventured an idea: "Maybe next time we should go when the snow is off the ground."

"Don't bother me," Dad replied. "I'm thinking, and what I'm thinking is that we need a new vision statement. You can do just about anything with a good vision statement. How about 'Semper Investigare, Nunquam Invenire'?" Dad thought he knew Latin from watching movies about Latin America.

"Sounds good, Norm," they said. "What's it mean?"

"It's Latin," he said. "It means 'Always Searching, Never Finding.'"

That being something they could live up to, the vote was unanimous.

In the Bible it talks about knocking and the door will be opened. I've met some folks for whom that is true. Folks who stumble upon the holy like children upon morels. But for every one of those happy finders, I've met a weary knocker. Lifelong seekers whose knuckles are bloody-raw in their quest for the divine.

Sometimes they come by to talk. They flop down in a rocker and ask why God seems silent. I never know what to tell them, other than to keep on looking, that God works at God's pace. I point out that sometimes good things come easy, but not usually. So it's a matter of persevering, of not discouraging, of organizing your life to increase your chances of finding.

I didn't learn that from the Bible. I learned it from my dad, while traipsing through light-dappled woods in search of the Holy Grail.

Exercise

One consequence of sedentary, modern life is that 73 percent of us are overweight. As I write this, I have to let my belt out a notch and unsnap my pants. My waist has increased three inches in six years, and I've gained fifteen pounds, most of it in my stomach, which makes me resemble a snake who's ingested a small mammal. Worse yet, my wife isn't overweight. I wish she were. Then she would pile food on my plate and say "Eat, eat!" like they do in those Italian movies. Instead, she flits around in a leotard exhorting me to exercise. Between you and me, I'd rather be fat.

When I was younger I exercised to build a muscular, chiseled physique that would attract young women. This has its equivalent in the animal kingdom with the fire-red cardinal and the strutting peacock. And it worked. Every time I went somewhere, flocks of birds followed me home.

Then I married and stopped exercising. You

probably think I stopped exercising because I'd managed to attract a mate and no longer felt it necessary to keep myself fit and attractive. You might be right. Whatever the case, I did not lace a jogging shoe or curl a barbell for twelve whole years. During that time, we had children. Doctors have long contended that bearing children causes weight gain. It's true! I've gained ten pounds since our children were born.

In the winter of my thirty-fifth year, I took up exercise. This I did at the urging of my wife, who pointed out that if I continue to expand at my current rate, I will weigh 475 pounds by my seventieth birthday. So three mornings a week I go to the basement and pummel myself into shape on a giraffe-like machine called a Nordic-Track. Next, I lift weights. After one month, a faint burp of a bicep has appeared. Then I come upstairs and eat three pieces of bacon, two bowls of Sugar Smacks, and a cinnamon roll. Plus I take a vitamin, proper nutrition being important to us fitness buffs.

Exercise, I'm discovering, is in no way fun. Its advocates speak in reverent tones of the post-exercise glow. All I feel is itchy and sweaty and achy. Exercise is the price we pay for inventing labor-saving devices. Our ancestors cut firewood by hand and chased their food through the woods. Sometimes their food chased them. Life was exciting back then, and people were a lot thinner, probably because of consumption. They also didn't smile when their pictures were being taken, but that had something to do with corsets.

The worst thing that happened for exercise fans was when Jim Fixx died. Remember him? He jogged a lot and went around the country telling other people what was good for them. Then one day his heart attacked him, and he died. His doctor said if he hadn't been exercising, he'd have died ten years earlier. That's the kind of thing you'd expect a doctor to say. I was hoping a doctor would come out and say, "If Jim Fixx had stayed home, watched TV, and ate butter pecan ice cream, he'd still be alive."

The Bible has a lot of exercise language in it. Paul speaks of the Christian faith as running the race and pressing on toward the goal, though I don't get the impression Paul was big on exercise. He was too busy getting knocked off horses and thrown in jail. I'm betting the exercise talk was Paul's way of reminding us that the Christian life requires no small amount of work and discipline.

Lot of talk these days about grace and how God loves and forgives us. I believe that. I also believe that while we live by grace, a daily dose of soul exercise never hurts. Besides, think of the benefits—if we're too busy praying, we won't have time to jog. Rats!

Misery to Joy

Every two years we hold a rummage sale at our church. It takes that long for the memory of the last rummage sale to fade. Then a widow needs some help or the meetinghouse needs fixed, and before you know it we're rooting through our closets, digging for treasure.

My wife and I can't donate much stuff to the rummage sale, since a lot of the things we have were gifts from our church friends. Folks get upset when they spend thirty dollars on a Madonna and Child cookie jar at Christmas and see you selling it five months later for seventy-five cents.

Right before our last sale, I read an article about how too many toys can be bad for children. I know it can be bad for their parents—my wife threw her back out carrying their toy chest. We decided we'd sell some of their toys at the rummage sale, so after they went to bed, we gathered up everything they hadn't played with for a while and took it over to the church. Then—and this will show you how smart we are—we took our children to the sale. Those church ladies play hardball. Made us pay full price to get those toys back.

While we were there, we bought some more stuff. Found a toaster from the 1950s. It works a whole lot better than the one we bought last year at Wal-Mart, which we're going to donate to the next rummage sale. We also bought a Tupperware cake carrier. We don't ever make cakes, but it was such a good deal we couldn't pass it up.

Someone donated a Flowbee, so we bought that, too. You hook it up to your vacuum cleaner, and it cuts your hair. The box said, "As Seen on TV." What they didn't show on TV is how your three-year-old runs screaming from the room when you switch on the vacuum cleaner. The Flowbee had only been used once. Brand-new, it cost seventy-five dollars. We paid five bucks, but it cost us another ten for the barber to make things right.

A guy in our church donated a set of barbells. I thought about buying those, because my wife has been telling me I need to start a fitness program. Personally, I think I'm in pretty good shape. They were going for ten bucks. I would have bought them, but I couldn't talk any of the church ladies into carrying them out to my car.

We sold our kitchen chairs. One of the church ladies bought them after I told her they were priceless antiques formerly owned by Abraham Lincoln. Actually, we bought them from Spiegel when we first got married. We didn't need them anymore, since we had bought another set of chairs at an antiques store the week before. Got a real deal on them. Believe it or not, they once belonged to George Washington. The dealer swore to it on a stack of Bibles.

We made eight hundred dollars. The best deal we got was when one of the church ladies said she'd donate eight hundred dollars if we promised never to have another sale. But I think rummage sales are a balm to the church's soul. Throw a group of folks together, pricing and sorting, and all the little rifts and cracks of the past year seem to fade in the fellowship. Nothing brings folks together like a misery shared.

The Bible is full of stories of shared misery turning to joy. Like when Paul and Silas were imprisoned in a jail cell and they were singing songs of praise. That's what trust in God can do for you. You can be surrounded by outward gloom but overflow with inward joy. That's why Paul and Silas were so happy. That, and having a built-in excuse for missing their church's rummage sale.

Taking Inventory

Read a magazine article not long ago that said middle age starts at thirty-five, which startled me, that being my next birthday. I took the test that accompanied the article, though I didn't need a test to tell me I'm getting older. The signs are all there. I need glasses to read, I eat more toast, and the other day I asked a teenager to turn down his music, but not before saying, "If you call that music." Plus, I'm losing hair on my head but gaining it in my nose. A friend asked me if I've been snorting Rogaine.

Despite these obvious drawbacks, aging has certain benefits I never anticipated, achieving a measure of contentment being one of them. When I was younger, I was consumed with the idea of being known. I aspired to a big pulpit in a big city making a big name for myself. What I've gotten instead is a small pulpit in a big city, making a lot of friends. Sometimes what we think we need isn't what we need at all.

Another thing I've appreciated about middle

age is my marriage. When Joan and I were first married, we argued a lot. Now that we've been married twelve years and have two children, we seldom argue. Mostly because we're too tired, but also because our priorities have changed. We're less concerned with our "rights" and more concerned with our "responsibilities." After all, relationship, in the end, isn't about getting one's way. What it is about, I'm not yet sure. Ask me in twelve more years.

As I've grown older, my understanding of happiness has changed. It used to take a new piece of furniture to make me happy; now if the boys are healthy and Joan and I go to bed sleeping spoons, that's about as good as it gets. When it takes less and less to be content, we're on our way to joy. I don't want you to get the idea that I'm super-holy or anything. I've just noticed that people who try hard to be happy seldom are. Besides, happiness based on things is fleeting—cars rust, and the cat coughs up a hair ball on the new couch. We're better off aiming for peace at the center.

The things that used to cause me worry no longer do. For a long time, I wanted everyone to like me and used to fret if they didn't. Now I'm less worried about the good opinion of strangers.

On the flip side, there are other people whose opinion of me has become all-important. Perhaps the most significant change in aging is whose opinion matters to you and whose opinion doesn't. If you've thought about this yourself, you'll know what I mean.

When I was younger, I was impressed by wealth, but not any longer. I figure that folks with money got what they were looking for. I'm looking for something different. Mostly what I'm looking for, besides a nose hair clipper, is to appreciate what I have and savor where I am. Some days I manage to do just that; some days I don't.

I write this at year's end, the obvious time for retrospection, a good time to commit to paper what it is I've learned. It gives me a feeling of progress to realize I'm not making the same dumb mistakes year after year. Part of this is because I need room to make new dumb mistakes, but it's also because through retrospection I learn what has worked and needs retaining, and what hasn't worked and needs releasing.

In high school, I worked at a grocery store. Every Monday we took inventory to find out what we had and what we lacked. So, too, in the Christian life, should we take regular inventory

of all we are and all Christ summons us to be.
This I'm learning in my middle years, in my
small pulpit in a big city, among all my many
friends.

Hardware Heaven

Rawleigh Baker owned the hardware store in Danville. He was also the local mortician. Our small town couldn't generate enough death to keep the Bakers gainfully employed in the funeral business, which is why they supplemented their income with the hardware store.

Rawleigh didn't make much money at the hardware store because he'd hire anyone who needed a job. A man down on his luck could wander in and five minutes later be tying on an apron and weighing nails. Rawleigh never hired a woman to work in the store, knowing most men wouldn't dream of asking a woman, "Now should I use a flat washer or a lock washer with this?" For the same reason, Mrs. Mingle never hired a man to work in her dress shop. This was back in the days when you could sensibly discriminate without getting sued.

One glorious feature of Bakers Hardware was that you could buy just one of what you needed. Not long ago I required one bolt to repair my son's bicycle, but had to buy a package of twelve bolts to get the one. I'll never use the other eleven bolts, but paid $2.50 for them and won't throw them away. I put them in my workshop next to a package of eleven screws. I've recently come across a small hardware store which sells individual nuts and bolts. When I'm feeling nostalgic, I saunter in, plink my dime on the counter, and order one bolt. The owner deposits it in a small paper bag, folds the top, and hands it to me with his wish for a good day. I wish every business transaction were as congenial.

Trust was operative at Baker's. If you told Les, the counterman, you had ten screws at three cents each, your word sufficed. "That'll be thirty cents," he'd say, "plus a penny for Uncle Sam." Rawleigh once hired a man who counted our purchases rather than take our word on them. This was an embarrassment and made us feel immoral, as if we'd been caught by the Reverend Taylor buying a top-shelf magazine at the Rexall.

Bakers took cash, check, or charge. By "charge" I don't mean MasterCard or Visa. I mean telling Les to charge it to your account, which you would settle at month's end. My days as a freewheeling spender began when I learned about charging. I was eleven years old and went into Bakers, picked up a pocketknife, and asked Les to charge it to my father's account. I felt terribly important scrawling my name on the bottom of the note. My days as a freewheeling spender came to an abrupt end when my father got the bill.

I came by my nickname at Bakers. I had gone there to buy some fence staples and, without knowing what they were called, asked Les where they kept the u-nails. He started laughing and asked me what a u-nail was. After that, whenever I walked in, he'd call out, "Here comes old U-nail!" That's the curse of being from a small town. I could go off and get a doctorate in nuclear physics, come back home, and still be known as the man too dumb to know what fence staples are called.

Baker's closed down a few years after I left home. One of those hardware chains long on lawn chairs and bolts-by-the-dozen moved in, and Bruce, Rawleigh's boy, didn't feel like doing battle. The new hardware store doesn't have wooden floors, and the counterperson doesn't call out your name when you walk in the door. They don't give credit, either.

Sometimes people ask me what I think

heaven is like. I tell them it has wood floors and you get what you need with a minimum of fuss. The counterman not only knows your name, but your daddy's, and can even recall when your mother was in high school and dated Herbert Riggle, who played center on the '53 team that won the sectionals.

Trust abounds there. And fellowship so warm and gracious you could linger forever—which you can.

Family Values

First, let me say that I am a big believer in the family. Our country is only as good as its families. I am for the family. In fact, I think everyone ought to belong to a family. Naturally, by "family" I mean one husband, one wife, and two children. If the wife can stay home with the kids that would be nice. And if they can live in the suburbs, that's even better. Just like on *Leave It to Beaver*. Now that was a family!

A lot of people think families are in trouble because women work outside the home. There's something to that, and I think Congress ought to hold a hearing on why we let it happen. If I remember right, this trend started with the advent of the outboard motor. Men, who had been content to stay home on the weekends and build birdhouses in the garage, wanted to spend weekends at the lake. But boats cost money. Lots of money. More money than most men make. So we encouraged our wives to enter the work force. They wouldn't have to earn a lot, just enough to buy a nice boat. Let's say sixty-seven cents to our dollar. So women started working, and everything fell apart.

My fellow Americans, our task is clear. If we want to restore family values, we are going to have do something about the rising cost of boats. What I propose is electing politicians with the courage and conviction to enact boat subsidies for the average American family. Instead of throwing all our money away on welfare, let's get to the root of America's real problem—skyrocketing boat prices! I think churches ought to get behind this. After all, Jesus spent a lot of time on boats.

Eventually, we're going to want to pass a law about garage sizes so that everyone will have enough room to store their boats. Nothing trashes a neighborhood quicker than a bunch of boats sitting around in driveways. So I'm looking for a politician who will promise to put a boat in every garage. And if you're serious about family values, you'll join my crusade.

Obviously, I'm kidding, except for what I said about boats costing lots of money. But some of the other solutions I hear seem just as silly. We require schools to teach family values. We demand that politicians legislate family values.

We even expect Hollywood to promote family values. Everyone is supposed to instill family values, except for families.

Let's take it from the top. Schools are here to educate. Politicians are here to govern. Hollywood is here to make money. But families are here to nurture, to love, to support, and (dare I say it?) instill values.

So how do we pass on values? We practice them as parents. Simple. But hard. Consistency is the key.

If you want to teach peace, model forgiveness.

If you want to teach abstinence from drugs, empty your liquor cabinet.

If you want to teach integrity, keep your word.

If you want to teach thrift, practice simplicity.

If you want to teach sexual purity, don't cheat on your spouse.

If you want to teach compassion, rein in your judgment.

If you want to teach mercy, be merciful.

And take your children to church—a good, healthy church where love and compassion are not only preached, but practiced.

Family values. They're free, but they cost. Even more than boats.